Our Spiritual Brain

Our Spiritual Brain

Integrating Brain Research and Faith Development

Barbara Bruce

ABINGDON PRESS / Nashville

OUR SPIRITUAL BRAIN
*Integrating Brain Research
and Faith Development*

Barbara Bruce

This book is printed on recycled, acid-free paper.

ISBN 0-687-09266-3

Library of Congress Cataloguing-in-Publication Data on File.

02 03 04 05 06 07 08 09 10 11—10 9 8 7 6 5 4 3 2 1

Manufactured in the United States of America.

To Ellen Arnold
coach, mentor, friend,
without whose support and confidence in me
this book would not be

Contents

List of Figures

Foreword

The Brain. We all have one. We rely on it for our every conscious and unconscious act. But do we understand it? Do we know how to use it well? And most of all, as educators, do we really know how to tap the brains of others?

I, like Barbara, am addicted to learning more about people's brains. I remember taking my first education course (in the early 1960's). When my distinguished professor started talking about how to teach, I naively raised my hand and asked if it would be helpful to first understand more about the learning process before we figured the best way to teach someone. I was informed that if I wanted to know more about learning, the rat mazes were down the hall.

I did what I was told and signed up for a course in the psychology of learning, where I did, in fact, learn how to get rats to run through mazes. But I never found a way to use anything from that course in setting up or running a real classroom with people instead of rodents.

Barbara, however, has provided a totally different response, one that incorporates a wealth of current knowledge about our magnificent brains and a wonderful assortment of brain-friendly applications that you can use in your classroom immediately. You will enjoy her invitations for reflection using a variety of brain research. You will find moments to ponder, points to argue, and much to substantiate what you already know from your experience as both a learner and a teacher.

Blessings be to Barbara for translating this heavy, scientific material into a readable, interesting, and thought-provoking book.

To support you on your brain-friendly journey, I offer you the following acrostic.

Take this:

Opportunity to
Understand current
Research on your

Special but
Plastic brain that makes
Innumerable connections in order to
Reinforce your own
Intelligences. Barbara's
Thinking is
Up to date and
All encompassing as she
Links research and effective

Brain-friendly
Religious education through
Activities that
Incorporate the maximum
Number of neurons.

—Ellen Arnold
author of
Brilliant Brain Becomes Brainy
and the series *MI Strategies for Kids*

Preface

I needed to write this book. I needed to put on paper all the information I have discovered about brain research in a concise and user-friendly package. Many people see "brain research" and back off, fearing it to be technical, confusing, and intimidating. In many cases it is. I have done my research carefully, however, with you and me in mind. I have also neglected technical and biological terms, except to give you an overall picture of how the brain functions.

Brain research is so fascinating! We are living in a most exciting time. We are on the cusp of new discoveries that have the potential to transform every aspect of human life. At a recent brain conference I saw a person's brain waves on a computer screen. To actually "see" the process of thinking and watch areas of the brain light up when information is introduced is truly incredible.

We can hardly pick up a magazine or newspaper and not see an article on the brain. But, most information is presented piecemeal and in a format that is not always easy to interpret or translate into practical use. My intention is to take this astounding information and to create a resource useful for educators, explicitly religious educators.

Brain research is about making discoveries. It is about learning how this most amazing organism works and how it influences every aspect of your life. As a religious educator, you need to know how the brain functions and how to translate that information into better, more usable lessons to help students continue, with depth and purpose, on their journey of faith. I want to help you understand that there are reasons learning can be presented in ways that make the learner zone out or tune in. Understanding how the brain functions provides reasons why what we do or do not want to do makes sense.

You will not need to make dramatic changes in what you are doing in your classroom. A basic understanding of a few guidelines and some simple changes in what you are already doing make a great difference in how your students respond.

Introduction

I have always been an educator. While other children played house, I played school. I later taught both in public school and in Sunday school with mandatory professional training and a lot of gut instinct.

The completion of a masters degree in creative studies added to my learning about learning (metacognition). Three years of exciting courses led me to a growing understanding of how to help students become more creative. This knowledge of how to re-ignite creative and critical thinking greatly expanded my quest for information on how to enhance learning.

Over a decade ago I discovered the work of Howard Gardner and others in the field of multiple intelligences. I sensed a new direction that made my teaching/learning explode with energy. Gardner provided the theory behind everything I knew to be true about how people learn. In essence we all learn differently. When we tap into the ways we prefer to learn, we unleash God-given creativity. The connection was made and my excitement grew as I combined training in multiple intelligences and creativity. These two concepts fit like a key in a lock.

In the last several years I have added yet another dimension to my knowledge. As I continued my quest for information on how people learn, I began to see extensive references to brain research. I was still eager to continue to expand my understanding of how people learn. Now I was beginning to see WHY tools and techniques work or do not work in the teaching/learning process. Everything I know about the process of teaching/learning makes sense when viewed from the standpoint of understanding how and why the brain functions. Brain research became for me the third side of the triangle of creativity, multiple intelligences, and brain research. (See Figure 1 on page 16.) I no longer teach any of these components alone. They support and enhance one another.

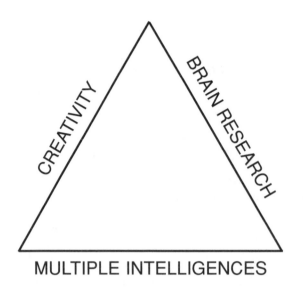

MULTIPLE INTELLIGENCES

Figure 1

I invite you to join in this research. As you read this book, use it as a work in progress with you as co-author. Check out the concepts. Test them on your students. Ask for their help as they reflect on what you are doing. Through such testing and reflecting we continue to make discoveries. It is called action research—the best and most informative type of research because you get immediate feedback from students who are actively involved in learning and growth.

Grace and Peace,
Barbara Bruce

How to Use This Book

Read / Reflect.
Test / Reflect.
Incorporate New Learning.
Test / Reflect.

The first section of this book is a brief background of the brain research that is fascinating so many people in so many fields today. This section is written for laypersons by a layperson. It is as free of jargon as it can be while still providing some basic information about the brain. I have included a glossary of terms and some graphics that many of us need to aid in our understanding. I have also included a section on brain theories and current reality.

The second section is about learning, particularly brain-based learning. We will consider how people learn, why people learn, and what the brain needs to make learning "take." Teachers and leaders who are interested in brain-based learning tend to have the interest of their students at heart. They believe in an active and participatory model, which includes students having a say in their own learning.

The third section is divided into twelve segments. Each segment is an application based on brain research. These applications may be incorporated into your teaching. Each of the applications may be used as a before, during, and/or after learning strategy. The applications are based on biological and neurological discoveries that translate into practical use for teachers and leaders.

At the beginning of each application is an exercise to help you become engaged with and to test your experience. At the end of each application is an "Action Research" worksheet for you to take notes, to write insights, and to record what you have observed from your students. Remember you are part of the action research of this book. By including your students in the process, you can both test the process and involve them in their own learning. Gone are the days "teacher" was in front of the room providing all the answers and being keeper of the information. A newer, more brain-friendly approach cites the teacher's role as facilitator of the process. Learning becomes a new adventure in which everyone wins.

My master's project was a follow-up study with managers of a large upstate New York food store chain who had participated in creativity training. Their response to the question "What constitutes a meaningful training event?" unanimously included the immediate application of what they had experienced. Their responses were variations of "A meaningful training is when I can take the information home and use it in my store tomorrow." That's what this book is about. Read the information. Reflect on what sense it makes to you in light of your experience. Read/Reflect. Then take the information and test it in your next class session. Involve your students. Tell them what you are about, and ask for their feedback. Test/Reflect.

This is not a book to put on your shelf to gather dust. Use it as a research tool to enhance and enrich your teaching/learning process. The next step is the reason the book was written: You can then incorporate your new learning into your teaching to enhance and enrich the understanding and faith development of your students.

The fourth section is taking your learning into new areas of discovery. Included in this section are

* suggestions for "brain breaks," strategies for brain stimulation
* suggestions for maintaining brain fitness and flexibility
* suggestions for parents and grandparents to help grow better brains
* a list of resources for further study—books, videos, Web sites

The Precedent That Drives This Study

You have a **spiritual brain**. There is no question that mind and body are connected in a single being that has been created for the glory of God. This concept is quintessential to who and whose we are. As you begin this study, read the words that provide the foundation for the journey you are about to take.

The Book of Discipline of The United Methodist Church, 2000, defines theology this way, "Theology is our effort to reflect upon God's gracious action in our lives" (page 74). Then it moves on to say that John Wesley, founder of Methodism, "believed that the living core of Christian faith was revealed in Scripture, illumined by tradition, vivified in personal experience, and confirmed by reason" (page 77). A brief sharing of the four elements as taken from the *Discipline* follows:

Scripture: "As we open our minds and hearts to the Word of God through the words of human beings inspired by the Holy Spirit, faith is born and nourished, our understanding is deepened, and the possibilities for transforming the world become apparent to us" (page 78).

Tradition: "The theological task does not start anew in each age or each person. Christianity does not leap from New Testament times to the present as though nothing were to be learned from that great cloud of witnesses in between. For centuries Christians have sought to interpret the truth of the gospel for their time" (page 79).

Experience: "Our experience interacts with Scripture. We read Scripture in light of the conditions and events that help shape who we are, and we interpret our experiences in terms of Scripture. All religious experience affects all human experience; all human experience affects our understanding of religious experience" (page 81).

Reason: "Although we recognize that God's revelation and our experiences of God's grace continually surpass the scope of human language and reason, we also believe that any disciplined theological work calls for the careful use of reason.

"By reason we

"read and interpret Scripture

"determine whether our Christian witness is clear

"ask questions of faith and seek to understand God's action and will

"organize the understandings that compose our witness and render them internally coherent

"test the congruence of our witness to the biblical testimony and to the traditions that mediate that testimony to us

"relate our witness to the full range of human knowledge, experience, and service" (page 82).

(These excerpts are taken from Section IV of "Doctrinal Standards and Our Theological Task" of *The Book of Discipline of The United Methodist Church, 2000*. Copyright © 2000 by The United Methodist Publishing House, pages 74–86, and online from the Library on the United Methodist Home Page—*www.umc.org*.)

Section One

Information

Just a bit of information to help you get an idea of what is going on in your brain—the most amazing bit of tissue in the universe.

We have learned more about the brain in the last three decades than in all of human history combined. You are born with 100 Billion (with a capital *B*) neurons or brain cells—give or take a few. Some of them will never be used and will die off or atrophy as you literally create your own brain. This amazing effect occurs as your brain forms itself out of your specific environment and needs. Not to worry, your brain keeps what it needs to make YOU who you are. We know it is not the number of brain cells we have that makes us intelligent; rather it is how we use them.

Some basic information—or a quick look at your brain

The human brain
* weighs in at about three pounds;
* can fit into a shoebox (men's size 13);
* is the shape of a walnut;
* has the consistency of butter;
* has an outer layer that is gray in color;
* is comprised of 78 percent water;
* is covered by a rumpled layer called the *cortex* (Latin word for "bark");
* has an outer protective shield—the skull;
* continues to grow and change through use and stimulation during your lifetime;
* differs between males and females.

(For more anatomical information about brain terminology, check the definitions in "An Anatomical Look at Your Brain," page 28.)

Humanity has been fascinated by the brain for thousands of years. Some people you may have heard of were fascinated with the brain and how it functions. Hippocrates (460?–377 B.C.), Plato (427?–347 B.C.), and Aristotle (384–322 B.C.) were all fascinated by ways in which the mind and body functions. Countless others were involved with theories of mind/body connections. Many scientists studied the brain and came up with innumerable theories. Some traces of their seminal work remain. Discoveries were made by probing the brain and observing what happened. Most of the studies were done on corpses or on people who had been brain damaged.

Today we are experimenting with many and varied ways of learning about the brain. New approaches to autopsies and hospital research, animal research, clinical studies in colleges and universities, phyto-chemicals, brain-imaging techniques, and action research provide us with useful and in some cases breakthrough information about the brain. Fascinating stuff!

Some of the most profound discoveries have been made in the closing decades of the twentieth century and the beginning years of the twenty-first century through the use of brain imaging technology. With the extended use of Electroencephalography (EEG), Computerized Axial Tomography (CAT), Functional Magnetic Resonance Imaging (fMRI), Positron Emission Topography (PET), Near-Infra-red Spectroscopy (NIRS), and Magnetoencephalography (MEG), we have added immeasurably to our understanding of what actually happens in the brain. Each of these imaging techniques works in a slightly different way to produce pictures of the brain. Some, like the EEG and CAT, have been around for many years and take X-ray-like images of brain tissue; some of the newest technology works to capture what the brain is engaged in doing. The still relatively new field of observing the brain as it functions has awesome potential. In the field of education alone think of the possibilities, including discoveries of learning differences and disabilities, ADD, ADHD, dyslexia, and the like. Researchers using imaging technology can scan a student reading and make discoveries about differences in comprehension when reading aloud or silently. Fascinating!

Brain research is one of the most rapidly changing fields of study. Blink your eyes and you may have missed something. Journals of medicine, science, psychology, physiology, and education to name just a few are replete with articles on the brain's functioning. *TIME, Newsweek,* and *National Geographic* ply us with cover stories on the brain. Women's magazines, sports magazines, and health and fitness magazines have jumped on board by making connections to body and brain. You can hardly read a national news magazine or newspaper or view much television without some mention of one of the fields of brain research. Welcome aboard!

Brain research is an interdisciplinary study. Coined *neuroscience,* it is composed of scientists and researchers from the fields of medicine, psychology, anthropology, biology, chemistry, philosophy, linguistics, and education. Each discipline is interested in discovering more about how the brain functions. Each discipline has its own agenda, its own need for data, its own applications. Perhaps one day the crossover information will be openly shared and met with enthusiasm and excitement in all fields.

Educators and philosophers, for example, have long been fascinated by the functioning of the brain. Over the centuries many theories of how behavior affects learning have been proposed. Most of them were based (in retrospect, perhaps implicitly or intuitively) on primitive brain theory and/or brain research. Some of these practices have stood the test of time, others served to open the door to possibilities, while still others became the latest educational flavor of the month. The one thing they have in common is a fascinating desire to learn about learning.

Education has its own "cloud of witnesses" who have provided us with glimpses into how to create optimal learning for children. Names like Jean Piaget, Maria Montessori, John Dewey, and Lev Vygotsky are among the pioneers who pressed for schools to look at the child and to teach to the child's needs.

John Dewey, an educational philosopher, was light years ahead of his time. He spearheaded the movement that became known as "progressive education"; which, over fifty years ago, was professing many of today's findings of brain research and learning. Dewey was among those who taught that hands-on education, teaching in the contexts of real events, was more powerful learning than using abstract concepts. He was opposed to passive rote memorization, standardized subject matter, and a uniform program of activities. He favored giving individual attention and consideration to each student, encouraging independent thinking and active community life within the learning environment. What a concept!

Behavioral scientists told us to increase productivity by rewarding positive behavior with treats or limiting unwanted behavior by punishing. We know this thinking is outdated. We also know now that the best motivation is intrinsic—coming from within. When students are ready and motivated to learn, it is almost impossible to stop them—no candy needed, thank you very much. When motivation is extrinsic—coming from external rewards—the information is learned to get the reward and then the information is discarded (think of a math test you took in high school; how much do you remember today?). We also now know that punishment does not always discourage unwanted behavior, and that punishment can discourage learning and cause emotional damage. The behaviorists worked on a theory that seemed relevant for their time; but with new information, this theory has now become outdated.

A major breakthrough came when Roger Sperry, J. E. Bogen, and others contributed theories based on findings from split-brain research. Briefly stated, the left brain and right brain house different functions. For many years educators incorporated this primary information into their understanding of how brain research and learning are connected. It seemed to fit with what these educators knew intuitively about differences in the way students learn. Although this seminal work opened the door to further and more involved research, we know that "right-brained or left-brained" terminology is now outdated. We know that similar functions can occur on different levels in either hemisphere. For learning to be complete, you must teach to both sides of the brain—the verbal and analytical as well as the artistic and emotional. Each hemisphere contributes to the learning; and seldom, if ever, is anything housed solely in one or the other hemisphere. (See Application 2, page 55, for further information.)

Edgar Dale created a visual for educators known as the "Cone of Learning" to help them understand that hands-on experience, actually getting involved, is the most productive form of learning. His model was used by educators for many years and still holds a great deal of truth. The truths Dale showed us have been expanded upon and updated to include new approaches to inclusive learning.

Dale's Cone of Learning

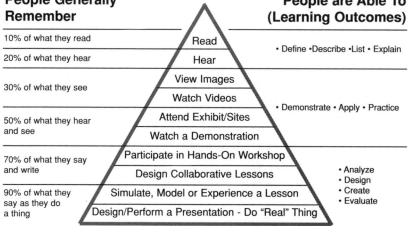

People Generally Remember		People are Able To (Learning Outcomes)

People Generally Remember

10% of what they read

20% of what they hear

30% of what they see

50% of what they hear and see

70% of what they say and write

90% of what they say as they do a thing

Read
Hear
View Images
Watch Videos
Attend Exhibit/Sites
Watch a Demonstration
Participate in Hands-On Workshop
Design Collaborative Lessons
Simulate, Model or Experience a Lesson
Design/Perform a Presentation - Do "Real" Thing

People are Able To (Learning Outcomes)

• Define •Describe •List • Explain

• Demonstrate • Apply • Practice

• Analyze
• Design
• Create
• Evaluate

Figure 2

Neuro Linguistic Programming, Whole Language, Learning Styles, Social Learning, and Multiple Intelligences are but a few of the many current "answers" to help students learn more completely through the connection of brain research and memory/education. Each of these theories adds to the overall information on learning. Each has taken the information gathered from examining the brain and how it functions, incorporated that information, and recorded and deciphered the results. Many of these answers have provided glimpses of the truth of how the brain functions; none of them has all the answers.

This book will focus on Multiple Intelligences. In my opinion, the most important contribution of Multiple Intelligence theory is that it has turned the world of education upside down by shattering the paradigm of intelligence being measured on a single dimension scale of IQ testing. It has rattled the cages of those who believe in the rarified world of Mensa—a society of people with extremely high IQ's. It has opened up a new and exciting time of honoring the gifts of people who excel in all walks of life.

Brain research is just that, research. It doesn't necessarily prove anything. But for educators, paying attention to the findings and testing them against their own experience and reality opens the doors for new and exciting possibilities to emerge in their teaching/learning strategies.

Brain research often raises more questions than it answers, which tells us that much more is yet to be learned. A wonderful and very visual model of learning applies here. It is a series of four steps:

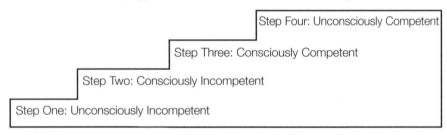

Figure 3

Step one is unconsciously incompetent—you don't know what you don't know.

Step two is consciously incompetent—you know what you don't know.

Step three is consciously competent—you know what you know but you have to consciously think about it.

Step four is unconsciously competent—you just do it without having to think about it—changed behavior or learning has occurred.

I believe we are somewhere between the consciously incompetent and the consciously competent stage in learning connections to brain research. We know many things. We know we are on the cusp of exciting breakthroughs and that there are many and varied ways to think about applying this new information. Also, ever newer information raises more questions and offers more challenges to practitioners. We are on the frontier of exciting possibilities.

Educators with inquiring minds want to know what all this research has to do with improving teaching strategies. How will this information (fascinating though it is) help students of all ages to learn and behave in more efficient ways? I hope this book will be one of the right answers in your search for meaning. You may find information repeated; I'm not simply being redundant. There are two specific reasons for the repetition: (1) Your brain will register this information in several contexts (educators have always known repetition is good), and (2) I have gathered my information from a variety of resources, in several disciplines. Each has something to share. Many overlap.

While we still do not have all the answers, I believe there are significant directions we can pursue. In the last two decades educators have linked brain diversity and uniqueness and multiple ways of learning with brain research and found reasonable and justifiable explanations for differences in learning abilities and needs. I believe these continuing areas of research will support integrating all areas of learning, including environmental considerations, cooperative learning, music and art, the understanding and use of emotions, mandatory reflection and feedback time, multiple right answers, creative and critical thinking, emphasis on quality above quantity, and experiential learning in which the students not only participate but have some control over what they learn. A lot to think about!

If you have a sense of fascination for this subject and would like more information than the micro version I have provided, see Resources, page 138.

An Anatomical Look at Your Brain

Some more in-depth anatomical information about your brain for those who want/need to know more.

Your brain

* has two types of cells:

> *Neurons*. Each neuron or brain cell (soma) has a sender (axon) and thousands of receivers (dendrites).
>
> *Glials*. Glials serve different purposes, among them the role of maintaining chemical balance and cleaning up brain debris. Glial cells outnumber neurons ten to one.

Two significant factors about neurons (brain cells) are different than the cells that comprise the rest of your body:

1. Neurons do not regenerate in the same way other cells in your body do. Researchers now believe there are differing ways that the body can create new neurons (more about that later).
2. Neurons communicate or transmit information. They do this through electrical and chemical signals. For the purposes of this book it is not necessary to get into the neural technology of how and why this happens. Check the additional resources if you want more in-depth information. What I have included in this text is the information that is important for you to have to make discoveries and change behaviors. You accomplish this by testing and including the findings from research in your teaching/learning.

* has a *cerebral cortex*, which is the complex layer that allows you to think and sets you apart from lower animals. The cortex contains four lobes in each hemisphere: *frontal* (located in the front of your brain—main function is processes thinking, decision making, focusing, reflecting); *parietal* (located at the top of your brain, divided into two sections—the anterior [front] processes sensory data and the posterior [rear] processes the data for spatial awareness); *temporal* (located just above your ears—main function is processing auditory data); and *occipital* (located in the central lower back of your brain—main function is processing visual data). Each lobe has a different function; but as in all brain

matters, they work together to create the process of disseminating information.

* has two *hemispheres—left,* which controls the right side of the body, and *right,* which controls the left side of the body.

* contains the *corpus callosum*, which connects the two hemispheres. This fibrous connective tissue allows information to cross from one side of the brain to the other.

* has a *cerebellum* (little brain) at the base of the skull, which is primarily responsible for movement and balance.

* has a *brainstem*, which is located at the base of the brain and connects the brain to the spinal cord and is responsible for actions that we do not have control over (breathing, heart rate, blood pressure, and so on). Some researchers suggest we can learn to control this through such things as biofeedback.

* has a *thalamus*, which controls the flow of information from the senses to the cortex.

* has a *hypothalamus*, which controls the normal state of the body as well as eating and drinking.

* has an *amygdala,* which essentially controls emotions.

* has a *hippocampus*, which holds immediate memory and sends it to the cortex where it is stored as long-term memory that can be retrieved at will.

(See Figures 4, 5, and 6 on pages 30–31.)

Medial View of the Brain

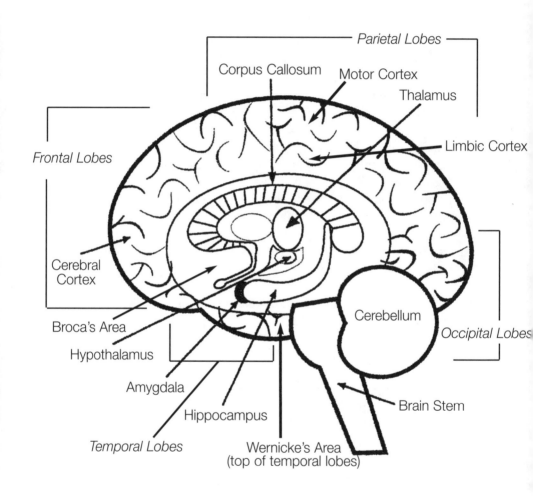

Figure 4

Neurons

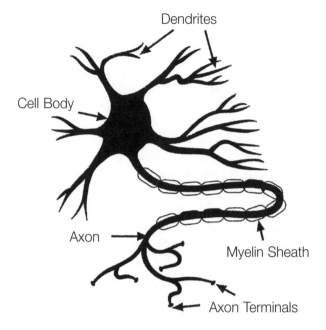

Dendrites

Cell Body

Axon

Myelin Sheath

Axon Terminals

Figure 5

Glial Cells

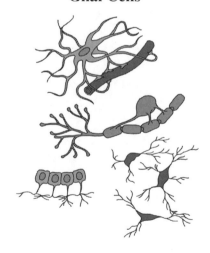

Figure 6

Section Two

Learning Is What the Brain Does Best.

Please take time to complete this page.

Think of the BEST learning experience you have encountered. Reflect on what made it the best. List everything you can think of that caused you to say it was the best learning.

_____

_____

_____

_____

_____

Now think about the WORST learning experience you have encountered. Reflect on what made it the worst. List everything you can think of that caused you to say it was the worst.

_____

_____

_____

_____

_____

There are reasons for both the best and the worst learning experiences you have encountered. *As* you read this book, you will make discoveries about the reasons for best and worst learning. Go back and mark the reasons in your best or worst list as you find reference to them in your reading, or check them as I have suggested at the end of each application. Learn from this experience and make the changes in your own teaching/learning.

Let's begin at the beginning. What do you actually mean when you speak the words "I remember"? The focus of this section is on what it means to remember something. It will answer two important questions: (1) How do you learn? and (2) How do you know you've learned?

Here are two simplistic answers to the questions:

1. You learn in many and varied ways and process your experience into long-term memory.
2. You know you have learned something when you can retrieve it from memory and/or your behavior is changed.

If you are not particularly interested in the details of how the brain functions, skip to Section Three for practical information based on brain research that you can integrate immediately into your classroom. If, however, you want to understand the intricacies of learning at a deeper level, read on.

A metaphor works well here. For educators, the basic metaphors of an auto mechanic or a driver deserve mention. You decide which fits you:

Auto mechanics have to have a working understanding of how a vehicle functions before they can attempt to make it run efficiently. You have to have a basic understanding of how the brain functions to help your students learn most efficiently.

Drivers simply spend time in the seat and steer. You can show up and follow a curriculum.

I sincerely hope you chose the auto mechanic. Helping students learn (not simply imparting information) is your primary task, your ministry. To facilitate learning at its optimum level, you must have a basic understanding of how the brain functions.

Memory making is a critical factor in how the brain learns. Since one of the definitive components of "learning something" is that you can understand it, store it as memory, and retrieve it, learning about how memory is used to create understanding is critical.

In this section you will find

* metaphors/models past and present to help you understand how the brain remembers/understands;

* a basic look at how your brain establishes memory for understanding;

* age-level suggestions for creating a foundation for memories that lead to understanding.

As a religious educator you need to know how and why your brain creates understanding and how it makes a difference in your teaching/learning process. Brain research answers get involved with what is actually taking place in your brain and throughout your nervous system. In order for learning to occur, a new experience must eventually be converted into lasting memory that has multiple links.

Tools to Guide Understanding

For a helpful explanation of how the brain creates lasting memory, test these similes, metaphors, and models. Similes and metaphors are helpful tools in making something that is complex more readily understandable. They are figures of speech that make an implied comparison between things that are not literally alike. Similes use the words *like* or *as* in the comparison: the Kingdom of God is like. . . . Metaphors simply make the comparison: Jesus said, "I am the bread of life." We know both of these figures of speech are powerful teaching tools. (See Application 2, page 55.)

Combining models with figures of speech adds another dimension to help you understand a complex concept by the comparison of two dissimilar things. The power lies in the fact that one of the things compared is a familiar quantity to you. Your brain makes the leap of understanding.

There are countless models and metaphors for how the brain functions with memory. Each of the following contains some truth. None is perfect.

Two metaphors involve memorization:

Plato believed the brain was like a *wax tablet* into which impressions were set. In this model/metaphor, the stronger the input, the deeper the learning. This metaphor led some early educators to believe that memorizing was paramount to teaching and a synonym for learning. We know this is not altogether true. While it is important to memorize some information—the multiplication tables for instance—in general memorizing information without a particular need for it is a useless, time-consuming, and boring exercise. Another example of useless information might be memorizing the names of the kings of Israel. This information is readily available if you need it for a specific task but otherwise serves no practical purpose.

A second popular metaphor is that memory is a *muscle*—use it or lose it. Just as with our physical muscles, our mental muscles must be kept active to maintain flexibility. It was thought that memorizing information or a series of facts would strengthen the "muscles" in your brain. We now know that part of the metaphor is true. You can keep your brain fit by using it on a regular basis to learn new information in order to keep the axons and dendrites sparking. Memorizing unimportant facts, however, does not necessarily serve the purpose intended in the metaphor. This kind of memorization causes frustration when you attempt to retrieve it, for this type of information does not get pulled into use very often. Therefore the brain does not consider it important, and it may have gotten stored away on some dust-collecting shelf of your brain where it is not easily retrievable.

Pierce Howard uses a *photographic* metaphor. He likens memory to a three-part process similar to developing a photo. You take the picture (immediate memory), develop it (short-term memory), and fix it with chemicals to make it last (long-term memory).

Jerry Larsen uses a *factory* model. He suggests your brain requires a warehouse of raw materials (memory), a manufacturing system (to turn memory and thought into actions), a shipping and receiving department (gathering data and sending it out), and a loading dock (short-term memory that is held until further processing).

A *computer* also has been widely accepted as a model for how the brain functions—what goes in is processed and turned into useful information. In your brain, data is entered through your senses, processed according to your needs, and stored as information that is readily accessible if you know the correct icons to click.

I do not relate well to these models. The part of the metaphor that is missing for me is the critical piece of the living, growing, and ever-changing aspect of the brain. Nonorganic metaphors cannot capture that essential aspect of the brain's amazing abilities, including memory.

For me, one of the most important pieces in understanding how the brain functions is that you have the amazing ability essentially to create your own brain. Everyone has a genetic makeup at birth that you cannot do much to alter. As an educator, however, you can play a part in the determination of the environment and experiences that mold and shape the brain. If you help students (of all ages) create positive experiences from an environment rich with the love of God and a good, strong value system, you will have established a blessed foundation for life experiences that follow.

Gerald Edelman uses a *jungle* as a metaphor—each organism is an integral part of a symbiotic relationship where everything stands alone yet depends upon everything else to function optimally. I like this metaphor because inherent in it is the concept of aliveness and the brain's ability to constantly reinvent itself.

Each of these models/metaphors has some validity, and many have faults. It's like the blind men describing an elephant, each thought the elephant "was" the part he described. Each had some of the information, but no one individual had the whole concept. Each of these models/metaphors has part of a truth, yet none can fully describe the amazing complexity of how the brain functions. The reason for using them is to help you compare something you know to something very complex.

A User Friendly Model

I would like to suggest a slightly modified version of the popular and widely used "Information Processing Model" as another metaphor for how the brain learns. It is not a perfect metaphor, but many researchers view it as a succinct, yet understandable picture of the way the brain functions. (See Figure 7, page 39.)

Basically, processing memory includes three steps: you get a stimulus—usually you see and/or hear, smell, taste, or touch something (sensory memory). This lasts for only seconds. The stimulus gets quickly sorted and processed by your brain (working memory). This step can take seconds to a few minutes. Once the route is decided, the brain does more sorting; and if the brain deems it important, it is stored in a way that the brain has the ability to retrieve it (long-term memory), which leads to understanding.

The first step in the learning process then is to receive input or stimulus from your world. You do this primarily through your senses—sight, sound, smell, taste, and touch—most often in multiple sensory experiences. Brain researchers know each of your senses can be extended into subgroups to create greater meaning. (More about this in Application 8, page 104.) Your senses are constantly at work in your environment collecting data. This data is held in your awareness (sensory memory) for fractions of a second until your brain decides what to do with it. If the data is not processed, it gets discarded. An example is riding down a highway and seeing a billboard advertising cars. You experience it through sight, but it is gone in the blink of an eye. Since it has no relevance to you (unless you want to buy a car, then your brain records the information), your brain filters it out with thousands of other passing images.

Your brain continuously sorts and processes the input in working memory. If the brain did not have this step, you would be inundated with so much sensory information that you literally could not function. All the sensory data that your brain deems important is transferred to the specific areas of the cortex that then individually and simultaneously process sight, sound, smell, taste, or touch.

This information is received as a perception by the brain. That is, this information is stored and processed based on what the brain already knows. If you see a dog, your brain automatically processes this sight with everything it knows about dogs. One person's perception might be to see a dog and run away because of a bad experience of being bitten by a dog. Another person's perception might be to stop and pet this friendly creature because the brain connects dogs to friendly, furry, occasionally noisy but harmless creatures. If you just landed from another planet and had never seen a dog before, this creature would have no meaning for you. Your brain would have no neural connections to "dog." Every sensory input is filtered through your brain's perception based on your experience. All this amazing filtering and processing happens in the blink of an eye and is known as pattern recognition.

This phenomenon explains why different people may have the same

Information Processing Model

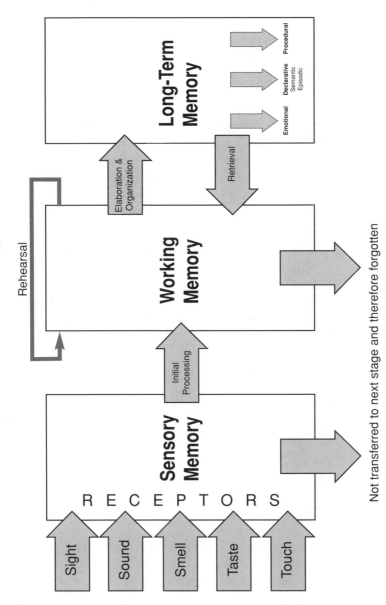

Figure 7

experience and yet react totally differently. I like dogs and have no fear of them. My walking partner, Paula, is terrified of them. If we saw an unchained dog on our daily walk, she would freeze or try to climb upon my shoulders. Our brains perceive "dog" very differently. This filtering and processing is done by your amazing brain without conscious thought from you. It is all based on pathways that have been established. Your brain makes "meaning" of your experience. You either connect it to something you already know, or your brain begins the process of creating new meaning and establishes new connections.

How then does the brain decide what is important and what to discard? The two most important determiners of what is important are: does it get my attention? and am I emotionally attached to it? Both are important factors in what your brain does next.

Your brain is designed to pay attention to those stimuli that have strong emotional connections. The part of your brain that processes emotions receives the information before (would you believe a quarter second!) the thinking brain. This may be the explanation of reacting emotionally before you react rationally. Your reaction to first impressions often sacrifices accuracy for speed. You act without thinking something through carefully. You might say it is a response of heart rather than head to the situation. The emotions also have a secondary, more thoughtful role. These emotions take longer (a few seconds) because they are formed in conjunction with thought processes, rather than immediate knee-jerk reactions. The complete explanation of how/where this happens would take a book unto itself. Suffice it to say that the brain knows where to put what to make it usable.

As a religious educator, this piece of information is critical to your teaching/learning process. Learning does not occur in a vacuum. Everything that has happened in your students' lives dictates how they will perceive your lesson. Some events have strong emotional triggers, some have minimal triggers; but all previous life events shape who your students are.

Once your memory gets hooked through attention and emotion, the brain sorts the stimuli in working memory into basically two categories: (1) Does this fit anything I already know? or (2) Is it new information? When a stimulus fits into one of those two categories, the brain deals with ways of processing it into long-term memory. Think of it as a fork in the road; your brain takes one of the two pathways from the initial stimulus through the route of working memory to the end station of long-term memory.

If it fits with something you already know, then a link is made. The stimuli reacts to established emotional pathways. The more these pathways get used, the more efficient they become. Learning thus becomes more efficient as well. Once the information is linked, it remains embedded in the brain and can be retrieved at will—from long-term memory.

Your brain actually uses less energy to make connections and to hook up to what you already know than to process new information. Through brain-imaging technology, we can see that less electrical or chemical energy is required to make well-known connections. This bit of information about memory points to the inclusion of Advanced Organizers. AO's are tools to help to make those connections in two specific ways: (1) They connect new information to what is already known, and (2) they help prepare the brain to learn.

If, however, the stimulus presents something unknown, then it travels to different sorting areas; and a new connection is created with the new information. Creating new connections requires more electrical impulses. Brain imaging technology records these electrical and/or chemical impulses as bright areas in the brain where new information is being processed. These lighted areas are involved with converting information into long-term memory. Once your brain decides this new information is worth keeping, it has several ways to incorporate it. If what your brain wants to remember is a person's name (Barbara), you can use many ways to imprint it. Repeating the name several times in your conversation helps to anchor it. A second way to imprint this new name is to make several associations. Barbara has green eyes. She is wearing a burgundy silk shirt and white skirt. Barbara said she is a teacher. Barbara has a firm handshake, and her voice has a pleasant pitch. Each repetition and inclusion of detail helps imprint the person on your brain. Think of the intelligences used in this exercise: Visual/Spatial (eye color, clothes), Body/kinesthetic (handshake), Musical/Rhythmic (pitch of voice), Verbal/Linguistic (said she is a teacher).

You need to connect new information to what you already know

AND you must keep learning new things to create new dendrite connections to stimulate brain fitness. When you introduce a concept the brain will follow one of these pathways.

Your brain works differently in each of these two processes. It takes less brain energy to process what you already know. Think of a time— we've all experienced this—when you leave church and pull into your driveway, without consciously being aware of how you arrived there. Your brain was essentially on automatic pilot, and you were using your brain to think of something else. But, if there had been a detour on your normal route, your brain would have had to focus, to work harder in considering alternative routes to get home.

One of the exercises for brain fitness suggests you consciously take a different route to make your brain work harder and to keep it fit. Actually switching any daily routine you do, like brushing your teeth or eating a meal, to your other hand causes your brain to produce more electrical charges and makes it work harder. Breaking routines in your classroom will serve the same purpose: more about that later.

In essence it is like learning to ride a bicycle. Think of how you learned to ride. The first several attempts took a great amount of energy, concentration, and focus. Many areas of your brain were working simultaneously—vision, balance, motor coordination, spatial awareness, and steering to specify a few. Once you learned how to ride, it became automatic. The neuropathways were formed, the connections made. It now requires little effort to function in this task—even if it has been years since you've been on a bicycle. It takes only a bit of input from one neuron (seeing a bicycle) to stimulate another, and the connection is made. Through a series of mind/body memories, your brain knows how to ride a bicycle. Isn't it miraculous? Lasting memory has imprinted an understanding of riding a bicycle. Barring any physical damage to your brain, you will always "know" how to ride a bicycle.

Long-term memory has several processes of accessing information. Basically you have these:

Procedural memory is your "how to" memory. This kind of memory allows you to go about normal routine processes without having to think about them. If you had to think about how to brush your teeth or drive to work or operate your keyboard, you would be so tied up in thinking about doing, you wouldn't accomplish anything. Once these activities have been practiced many times, they become reflexive, automatic, unconscious acts and are stored as procedural long-term memory. You can retrieve them without thinking.

Emotional memory is the filtering system of all of your memories. Everything you remember has some emotional basis to it.

Declarative memory requires some reflective thinking. You need to consciously recall something. Declarative memory is then divided into two types:

Semantic memory, which helps you remember all the rules of grammar and how to construct paragraphs. It helps you remember facts and general knowledge. Knowing the Lord's Prayer is an example of semantic memory.

Episodic memory, which helps you remember your first church and favorite Sunday school teacher. It helps you remember events and people in your life. It may help you remember who taught you the Lord's Prayer. Episodic memory is culled from many areas of your brain; and since we know information is filtered through perception and emotion, these memories may be less accurate. Remember the song from *Gigi*, "I Remember It Well"? This wonderful song, sung by Maurice Chevalier and Hermione Gingold, captures this classic concept. Each of them recalled their early courting differently.

I'm sure this has happened to you. You are discussing a common event with a friend, and each of you remembers it in a slightly different way. Episodic memory holds the event and the details may become fuzzy because your memory is shaped by your emotions.

In summation, learning becomes easier when you connect it to something you already know, when the neuropathways have been established. When these connections have been made, they must be reinforced to maintain meaning. (See Application 2, page 55.) You know you have learned something when you can retrieve it from long-term memory and use it at will.

Learning becomes more brain stimulating when new information is introduced. New neuropathways must be established. This process simply means the brain has the (amazing) ability to re-form itself with new information. What a blessing!

This important information has tremendous impact on learning. You have the power at your command to help students successfully travel their journey of faith and make life-changing decisions. Students make these ethical and value-centered decisions when they are introduced to new concepts. New neural pathways have to be created. They can also make these decisions when they have a rich background of experiences to draw from. You can prepare an environment that is filled with a quality and a quantity of theological concepts. You can create memories or call upon memories to guide your students into making discoveries of their personal relationship with God. It is an awesome responsibility.

Age-Appropriate Suggestions for Creating Memories

How do you go about creating a rich environment from which to draw memory? This question requires different answers at different ages. For the purposes of this book, I will address the issue from the standpoint of religious education. (Visit Section Four for more general information, page 129.)

For *young children*, create a place of love and safety. When young children begin to associate with church or "God's house," let it be with warm feelings of being loved and cared for because the brain functions best in an environment that is safe and nonthreatening.

In God's house you tell biblical stories of God's love in age-appropriate language because the brain is storing words in semantic memory. You provide visual symbols—a Bible is a book of stories about God and people, our cross represents Jesus' life, water is about baptism and becoming part of God's family. You do this to imprint sensory information in the brain. Your room needs colorful pictures and objects to create visual stimulation because the brain is imprinting and storing these images. It needs safe and exciting playthings to explore to help develop procedural memory of how to get around and about.

Most of all this learning place needs you. You are the one who knows each child by name and who takes time to engage in age-appropriate conversation. You are the one who listens to tales of bandages on hurts and new shoes. The environment should speak loudly and clearly of love and caring. I tell my nursery and preschool teachers, "Your primary ministry is to make certain that children know they are loved and cherished by God and by you." The brain flourishes in the chemicals that are produced by comfort and pleasure.

Many young children associate the pastor (especially if he or she wears a robe) with God. Their need for concrete meaning puts a literal figure with an abstract concept because the brain needs to create meaning. Young children also see their teacher as an ultimate authority figure. One of the parents came to my office after Vacation Bible School and laughingly said, "Madison thinks you are the authority on everything; and frankly we are getting tired of hearing, 'Barbara Bruce says. . . .'" Be careful what you say and do. You are creating memories that may last a lifetime. (See Application 1, page 50, for more detail.)

God's love and your love for children continues as an ongoing theme. *Older children* begin to recognize stories and to develop a foundation for learning about who and whose they are. This happens as you create positive emotional memories. They begin to make associations. As children enter elementary grades, they begin to hear the biblical stories through their curriculum. More important, they hear and see faith modeled by those given the responsibility to teach and lead them. The age-old adage "faith is caught rather than taught" is alive and well. Teachers can make a monumental difference in the way children see God. You create meaning that will carry them through early adolescence when they begin to question and make more abstract discoveries.

Children hear the stories of faith. You can make these stories truly meaningful by connecting them to what we know about how the brain creates and uses memory. You repeat these stories on a curriculum cycle, which enables children to hear them several times and at a variety of faith development levels to help strengthen neural pathways. Children need to experience stories of faith in a variety of ways in order to imprint the information at several areas in the brain. Each story should be connected directly to the life of the student to ensure that his or her personal background knowledge is tapped. Meaning is made when you connect what you already know to something new. Each story should be rich with sensory detail: what did it look like? smell like? taste like? sound like? You incorporate these details to make sure many sensory pathways for input are triggered. Objects connected to the story and other tactile and kinesthetic experiences are used to make connections of mind and body.

Reflection time should be included in every lesson to ensure the brain has time to imprint the material and to revisit the neural pathway that has just been established. Ethical and moral teachings are interwoven into the lessons as a foundation for decision making to incorporate critical thinking skills by stimulating the cortex. Incorporating stewardship, both personally and globally, is a basic concept—we are to care for God's creation. Living the Golden Rule is a part of each lesson, if you want to make sure it becomes a life-long concept. Saying grace before a snack develops habits of thanksgiving. Habits are created when you reestablish a memory connection. Make life-long memories for the brain to feed and grow on.

Youth have a more complete memory bank than children, but their brains are still developing certain skill areas such as intrapersonal thinking. This is a critical time in the life of a child of God. Their very personhood is at stake. Since the brain and body cannot be separated, you must create opportunities for praise (see Application 1, page 50) and must not tolerate breaking the Golden Rule. Sunday school and the youth group may be the only safe place for the emerging spiritual "being" of a youth. Make it a sacred place by providing memories that are imprinted in the brain through positive emotional experiences. Often youth look back at the experiences of a youth group as life-forming or life-changing.

Many youth engage in mission and service projects. Experiences like these are more than simply a good idea. They are memories built on experiences of living out God's love in the world. My daughter was blessed with the opportunity to travel to the Soviet Union on a "Mission of Peace" trip in her junior year of high school. The youth met with Soviet youth in their homes and churches to make personal connections. They got to experience a microcosm of the world and found more similarities than differences. When we met her returning plane at two o'clock in the morning and asked about the trip, her reply was, "It was the best two weeks of my life." That trip gave her a memory base that will always remain with her. Take advantage of this memory-forming time. Make it a positive foundation for life-long values.

Adults arrive with a lifetime of memories: some good, some quite awful. All their memories make the sum total of who they are. Their selfhood is wrapped up and neatly or haphazardly packaged in their memories. This is a rich tool for teaching and learning.

One of the decisions the brain makes within seconds of an experience is, does this connect with something I already know, or is it new information? The brain functions differently depending upon the answer to that formative question. An obvious conclusion is that since adults have such a deep memory bank to draw from, the brain will almost certainly use the function that fires up those pre-existing connections. Provide ample opportunity for faith sharing. Encourage adult students to witness to God acting in their lives. Each time they tell a faith story, it becomes more deeply engraved in the fabric of their being. Each time their emotions are triggered, learning is enhanced.

Memorizing is not altogether bad. Memorizing the Lord's Prayer or Psalm 23 or a favorite creed may be helpful and comforting. I attended a large funeral some years ago. When the pastor asked those gathered to join her in saying the Twenty-third Psalm, not many Bibles were opened. We knew it by heart. To hear nearly three hundred people recite this rich and meaningful psalm was a moving experience. The fact that most of us knew it "by heart" spoke volumes about the faith of the community gathered to celebrate this woman's life. Other good examples of memorization are the countless stories of prisoners of war who relied on their memorization of Scripture to help maintain sanity during their incarceration. Many older adults who were brought up memorizing Scripture find it comforting and helpful during the dark nights of their souls.

Take advantage of the wealth of information wrapped up in each adult. Invite adults to share memories connected to your lesson in the total group, small groups, or pairs prior to your lesson. This preteaching exercise will prepare the brain to learn your lesson by warming up the dendritic pathways.

Section Three

The Brain Has an Amazing Ability to Grow and Change.

Faith is as much a matter of head as of heart. The two cannot be separated. Blind obedience to ritual is not faith. In John Westerhoff's "stages of faith," he talks about questioning faith as an important step on your spiritual journey. It is important to think.

This book is about thinking and reasoning and making your own discoveries about who and whose you are. This section is about the practical application of brain research in your classroom.

Some scientists do not believe there is a direct correlation between brain research and learning. Some scientific researchers are loath to make any inferences without years of trial and error, hypothesis testing, and critical evaluation. We may lose another generation of students by then. As an educator, you are the judge of what these findings say about your students and your classroom. As an experienced educator, I believe they speak volumes.

Each of these applications is based on brain research and may be incorporated into your teaching at any time during a lesson. Each of these applications can be used to make taking steps along the journey of faith more enjoyable, more rewarding, more understandable, and, most important, more meaningful. These applications have power to stimulate thinking, to imprint thinking, and to reflect on thinking, all of which are important in the learning process. Mix and match depending on your students and the spiritual content to be studied.

Application 1

A safe environment is key
to maximized learning.

Try this exercise: Close your eyes and recall a time when you felt fearful and/or threatened in a learning situation. Perhaps you had not read the assignment and were afraid of being called on. Maybe you were not certain your answers were as good as someone else's and you might set yourself up for ridicule. How did you react? Were you paying attention to the content being presented? Or were you focusing on your fear and becoming anxious and stressed?

An article that I read on adult learning stated that adult egos play a significant part in learning. Many adult egos are sensitive to criticism and negative comments on their performance. Very true. But, the truth is not limited to adults. Students of all ages are vulnerable to paralyzing (negative) and crystalizing (positive) occurrences, comments, or events the brain has recorded.

Think of a time (any time) in your life that you have had a negative statement made about you that has remained a part of who you are from that moment on. I can't sing. I know I can't sing because Mrs. Goldman told me I couldn't sing. She barred me from the choir when I was in third grade. I have carried that paralyzing experience through most of my life. Last year, however, I sang the chorus of "We Need a Little Christmas" as part of a sermon. What a breakthrough! But it took me many, many years to dispute that brain message. You can damage an ego of any age with criticism, put downs, or negative comments. Be careful what you say.

By the same token, think of a time when someone praised you. Praise, too, is recorded in your brain and provides information on who you are. When you tell a child (or a person of any age) he or she is terrific, special, or wonderful, those "tapes" remain as well. They become part of that person. I have a friend who received praise for everything she did as a child. In her adult years, she has a good sense of self-esteem; and her brain is still wired with that information. What a gift and a blessing you can give! Take every opportunity to tell children (little and big) how wonderful they are and how proud you are of them. Look for things to praise, and students of any age radiate.

Statistically, it takes a four-to-one praise-to-criticism ratio to keep students on track. To improve learning, you need to up that ratio. This has nothing to do with false praise. Praise is genuine appreciation of any detail. Statements such as, "Your hair looks great," "I love your smile," "You bring joy to this class," "I appreciate your listening" all work to enhance a person's sense of self-worth when done honestly. Praise floods the brain with chemicals called endorphins that lead to a sense of well-being. Try it. Encourage your students to practice honest praise. Watch the results. As part of the action research, ask for student response.

As a rule we do not offer praise, and many do not know how to graciously accept it. Yet, it feels wonderful and has the power to communicate acceptance and love. Isn't that what Christian education is all about? You cannnot teach God's word completely in the absence of love.

To integrate this brain research finding into your classroom, remember that creating a safe environment is not simply a good idea; it is critical for any significant learning to happen. We know the brain produces a hormone called *cortisol* when it feels threatened. Cortisol is responsible for what is known as the "fight or flight response." This was and is very important in terms of dealing with danger. But when students feel threatened in a learning situation, cortisol remains in the bloodstream for an extended period of time. This chemical can cause damage to the hippocampus, the area of the brain involved with memory. Damage to this area impairs learning.

In most Sunday school classes we do not experience severe threat, but . . . fear of ridicule or being called on for answers or to read aloud can cause similar psychological damage to occur, and therefore learning is impaired. A psychological threat that is perceived is just as real as a physical threat. We know that perception is reality. Your brain does not distinguish real threat—someone appearing with a gun—from perceived threat—fear of being asked to speak in public. To your brain, threat is threat and the brain reacts.

If you want students to learn in the greatest depth, you must assure them and covenant with them that they are safe emotionally and physically in this place. There will be no ridicule. There will be no put downs. You will not require them to stand and recite answers. Their opinions and ideas are acceptable because they come from people who are respected and cared for. This does not mean you all have to agree. It simply means everyone tries to keep an open mind and heart. If your ideas are trampled, consider how likely you are to venture another answer. Only the bravest souls will test that water again.

In the church, which should be a home of love and acceptance, we often find theological differences. We are all on a faith journey. Most of us are in different places. To get across the idea that each place on that journey is acceptable to God is a critical piece in your teaching. To place God in a box that only allows one (true) belief is to place our human limitations on an awesome and infinite God.

Often, however, total acceptance is not the case. There will be differences based on scriptural knowledge, life experience, previous church involvement, or lack of church involvement. The church has both a right and left wing, previous members of another denomination that come with religious baggage, biblical literalists, and the biblically illiterate. God blesses them all. The critical question is, can we get along together in a Christian classroom? The simple answer is YES, with God's help. The second right answer is YES, if you are aware of the consequences of embarrassment and ridicule and take all possible precautions to keep the learning environment safe.

You, as facilitator, must be a role model and establish the guidelines. You must set the environment of acceptance and love. You must put a stop to any ridicule the first time it happens. Include your students in establishing ground rules, but you set the example of dealing with them. If your students have had a part in creating the ground rules, they can also be responsible for holding one another accountable; but you are still the role model. If you model the nonacceptance of negative behavior, so will they. Make it fun as opposed to a sense of punishment, but get the message across. It will only take one or two instances and the message will be received. You may rescue someone's ego and protect the fragile self-esteem of someone's brain.

If you have someone who continually abuses the ground rules, you may have to take that person aside in private and say that he or she may well be damaging the psyche of another of God's children.

Take some time and invite open sharing of paralyzing or crystalizing experiences (we've all had them). This helps students to recognize their own experiences and to hear the stories of others in the class. It will be time well spent, and you will create a brain-friendly environment.

Several studies have been done on what stress does to the brain as well as to the body. While you constantly deal with little stresses, when you come across a big one (for you) your brain and body react. When your brain senses threat, the cerebral cortex or learning brain is shut down by a chemical reaction. The brain's survival mechanism kicks in, and learning gets placed on a back burner. Also, when a person is under severe stress over a long period of time (real or imagined), the chemicals that the brain produces can cause severe damage to the body including backaches, migraines, chest tightness, and allergic reactions. Some of the most common causes of stress are worry, anger, discouragement, self-consciousness, embarrassment, or shame. Before the brain can deal with learning, stressful threats must be eliminated.

A good rule to follow: First eliminate stressful threatening situations to your best ability; then work to create an environment that encourages praise and compliments.

Action Research

Be certain to engage your students in your research.

How do you create your learning environment?

Record your stories of paralyzing or crystalizing events.

Discover the stories of your students. Record them.

Record your class ground rules.

How will you handle students who break the rules?

How might you produce a safe environment before, during, and/or ending your class session?

How might you respond to studying Scripture if you were being harassed or threatened with severe punishment for doing so? Ask your students for their thoughts as well.

Check page 33 to see if anything dealing with threat or fear of embarrassment appears on your worst learning experiences list.

Application 2

The brain is designed
to create meaning.

Try this exercise: Close your eyes and recall a time when you entered into a situation that you knew little or nothing about. You had no idea what was expected of you, what you were looking for, what you were supposed to accomplish. Fortunately, those experiences in the extreme are few. But if you have ever experienced something along those lines, try to recall what was going on in your mind and body. Most likely you became tense, frustrated, anxious, and/or nervous. Your brain wanted/needed to create meaning.

The brain has changed over the thousands of years of human history according to human need. One of the brain theories that was espoused for many years was the Triune Brain Theory. In essence, it was believed that the brain contained three sections: the reptilian brain (the most basic brain designed for survival), the mammalian brain (which housed emotions), and the neocortex or thinking brain (which caused us to reason, sort, problem-solve, and create meaning). While most researchers believe this theory is too simplistic, we do know the brain developed as needs arose. Early humans relied on their brains to avoid danger and to provide life-sustaining needs. Early on it was accepted that emotions played a significant part in how humans function. As humans have evolved as a species, we needed to expand the meaning created by the brain. Today, you need to think and respond to thousands of stimuli daily. Your brain must make sense out of all this chaos. That is what it is created and has been formed to do.

One of the ways you can help your students create meaning is by using advanced organizers (AO). An advanced organizer is just that, a method of arranging data prior to learning to help the brain create meaning through emotional or sensory cues. Creating these connections is necessary *before* you introduce meaningful content. In order for meaning to be complete, you need to make emotional and sensory as well as contextual connections.

Advanced organizers come in many shapes and forms. They all serve the same purpose: to hook up an emotional or sensory context for immediate learning. How you set up your room can be an AO. If you are studying the healing of the paralytic (Mark 2), you might have bandages and a stethoscope or a picture of a stretcher and a picture or model of a pallet (two sticks with fabric stretched across). Have the items located in such a way that as soon as students enter the room, their senses and/or emotions are engaged with clues about their lesson. Pictures depicting a home in Jesus' time will stimulate the brain to make the connections of the differences between homes then and now and help students get into the story. Emotions connect to "home" as a specific place; visual or tactile clues stimulate the brain through many dendrite connections.

You might have a question written on a chalkboard or on poster-board, such as, "When have you believed in something so much that you were willing to take a risk for your belief?" A question like this stimulates the brain by tapping into emotions to make connections to what it already knows and sets up the learning experience.

You might post a simple agenda. Some students *need* to have an agenda posted. For them, it helps the brain to know what is coming. Part of their brain's organization for learning is to mentally check off what has happened and to know what is expected to happen. They are sequential learners. They must have a glimpse of the big picture before they can make the individual pieces fit. They must put things in order (both the agenda and the lesson) for learning to be complete. The way their brain is wired makes this sequencing a necessary part of learning.

Yet another type of advanced organizer is to post a main idea and objectives. Some students will learn better if they know what the expected outcome of their learning is (others will not even realize it is posted). They want to know what they are supposed to learn from this experience. This will help them understand why they are doing the things that are required to make learning happen.

An example for your lesson might be:

Main idea: Jesus used acts of faith to teach.
By the end of today's lesson students will
* experience the Scripture of the healing of the paralytic (Mark 2)
* discover and discuss at least two acts of faith in the Scripture

* explore their own healing and faith issues

Again, this helps the brain focus on what is going to happen. The brain is more adept when it knows what to look for. Good teachers write objectives when they prepare to teach lessons. Why not share your intentions with your class members? Why not include them in the learning process? Remember this is an action research project.

When I lead a Bible study, I provide my students with discussion questions and invite them to read the Bible background before they begin the daily reading. To a person, they have said this helps tremendously in their ability to focus more intently on their study. The brain is designed to create meaning. If your goal is to help students make the Bible a living document for use in daily life, then you must help students learn at a deeper level. It makes sense to provide tools to aid in brain function. (More about brain focusing later.)

You might ask what your students already know about the subject of your lesson. Unless you are teaching very young children, seldom does one come to the lesson without any information. This technique establishes an emotional connection and strengthens neural pathways. You can record their information on posterboard or a chalkboard. Be sure to record all information, even that which is incorrect. What you are doing, in effect, is giving students a pretest without using the word *test*, which may cause anxiety in some of your students. This technique focuses the brain on the subject at hand and prepares the brain to link new information to already known facts. It also helps to uncover misinformation. This is an important factor. When you attempt to build new learning on misinformation, it does not fit and may lead to further misunderstanding and/or frustration. Children and youth act out; adults opt out when they are frustrated.

Other types of advanced organizers are listening to music, providing objects to handle, wearing a costume, doing a drama, or watching a video clip. You might announce next week's Scripture so students have the week to read, go online if they choose, or simply think about it during the week. Anything that helps the brain prepare for the lesson is a bonus for enhanced and enriched learning. All these techniques help the brain create meaning.

Do not stop at the beginning. Keep the brain focused throughout the lesson; the brain learns more efficiently this way. As you proceed into the heart of the lesson, provide your students with a question or two (no more than three questions, please) to focus on prior to presenting the content. Remaining with the Mark 2 story, ask students to look for evidence of faith or to think about how this story might have actually happened or how it is happening today—metaphorically or in reality. When you introduce focus before reading, doing a drama, watching a video, or however you present material, the brain keys in on the information you desire; and meaning is self-discovered.

Your brain makes more significant discoveries when it knows what to look for. You have seen many examples of this phenomenon in textbooks and magazines. For our purposes, a classic example of this concept is the word *Jesus* written in negative space.

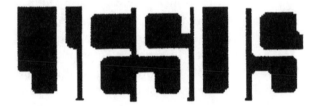

Figure 8

At first glance many people cannot make any meaning of the word. Once they are told what to look for, it is almost impossible not to see the word. The brain has recorded the picture.

Another set of tools are called graphic organizers (GO). We know that the brain understands more information if it is presented in a visual format. The brain "sees" through several areas and more dendrites are fired up. Mind Maps, Venn Diagrams, flow charts, ladders are but a few of the ways you can help students organize information you are presenting. When material is presented in a graphic way, it helps the brain to "see" the story as well as to hear it. For the healing story, you might have students list the participants, list the important facts (as on a ladder), or create a flow chart of what happened when and the cause/effect it had on those present and on the reader. Create a mind map with Jesus in the center and friends, paralytic, listeners, homeowner, Pharisees, around the edges. Combine the participants with lines of similar feelings. Another form of graphic organizer is a "see/hear/feel" chart.

These graphic organizers serve the brain in at least two ways: (1) they help the brain organize the information—remember, the brain exists to create meaning; (2) they present a visual picture so that an additional sense is incorporated into the learning and learning is diffused rapidly over a greater area of the cortex.

Yet another way of helping the brain create meaning is through engaging emotions. Emotions (positive or negative) provide the filter through which your brain receives information. (See Figure 7 on page 39.) For normally functioning people it is impossible to separate brain and emotions. We are holistic beings. It is a huge mistake to attempt to eliminate emotions from learning. Bible study without emotion is like a lake without water—dry and barren, without its essence. Jesus was emotional. According to Scripture he wept (John 11:35), he celebrated (John 2:1-11), he got angry (John 2:13-16), he was compassionate (Mark 5:21-43), and he prayed with intense emotion (Luke 22:39-44).

Think of your emotional states in your relationship with God and Christ. Have you ever wept with God? Have you ever been angry with God? Have you ever invited God to your celebrations? Have you ever turned to God with compassion? Most people can answer with a resounding Yes. God is part of who you are, as close as the air you breathe. Why then would anyone consider keeping emotions separate from learning about God?

Get emotional in your teaching/learning. Watch what happens!

Often this type of emotional engagement will lead to tears. Oh dear, what do you do if someone cries? You deal with it. Depending on the situation, you let the person cry alone, or you offer a hand or a hug. If your student's tears seem too much to handle, you as leader escort the student out of the room and remain with her or him. The other class members will fend for themselves. Sometimes someone in the class who is close to the student might go with him or her. Much of how you deal with tears is age related. Children, youth, and adults may cry for very different reasons.

Once, when I was leading a women's retreat, one of the participants ran from the room in tears. Another woman immediately followed her. The remaining women in the group assured me it was under control, that the two women were close friends. I felt the situation was in hand and I would be an intrusion. The two women remained out of the room for nearly thirty minutes. When they returned, there was a sense of peace and tranquility about the tearful woman. She spoke to me later and thanked me for providing a safe place and a sense of catharsis. Something we did in our scriptural exploration triggered a response that led to her tears, her final acceptance of the situation. When we connect emotionally with God through exploration of God's Word, amazing things happen. Sometimes you cry.

Returning to our study of Mark 2, think of a time when you or someone you loved was very ill. Let yourself return to that time and feel the emotions that were present. Think of your prayers. Think of your fears. Think of what you might have done if Jesus had been in your town during that time. Would you have found a way to reach him, even if you were told there was no room in the house?

Linking to an emotional time in your life helps the brain to make connections and to get all those axons and dendrites sparking and preparing to add more information to an already known quantity.

In a similar vein, you can help your students create meaning by connecting the biblical story to personal life experience. Emotions are a powerful way to connect. Every memory has some emotion attached. Not all of them are equal in depth. Some connections elicit joyful emotions, some pleasant, some annoying, some sorrowful, some fearful, some angry. Each of them strengthens the brain connections. Each human emotion has been experienced before. All emotions are present in Scripture. Connecting God's story to your story is often referred to as "Bible to life."

This connection can also be made by asking your students to think of an experience in their life, focus on it, recall it in detail, and then connect it with a comment like, "Scripture deals with a similar experience; listen now for how early Christians dealt with a similar experience." This is called "life to Bible." Depending on the circumstances, either of these methods is brain powerful. The biblical story takes on new meaning and is richer and fuller because your students have made the brain connections between their lives and Scripture. The biblical story takes on life and meaning. It is no longer simply words on a page or chapters in a book; Scripture becomes alive.

You can help the brain to create meaning by eliminating unclear terms. If there are gaps in understanding or initial misinformation, the brain becomes confused, connections cannot be made, and chaos begins to reign.

I was listening to a fascinating keynote speaker at a regional training event. His style was wonderful and his topic exciting. Then he used a word that I did not know the meaning of. I was lost for a few minutes. My brain was focused on trying to figure out what the word meant, and I missed some of his talk. I approached him at the end of the session and asked for the meaning of the word. He explained and said he knew as soon as he used it that he should have explained its meaning.

Often words are used in a presentation (or sermon) that are jargon or that have specific scholarly meaning to the presenter but leave the audience in a quandary. If you are using unfamiliar words, explain them; or be a role model by listing words in your lesson that you found unfamiliar. Invite your students to do the same. Keeping a Bible dictionary on hand is a great help in clarifying meanings. If your students do not understand a word or phrase, they miss the brain connection to something familiar and become frustrated and lose interest in the content. The brain is struggling to make meaning and not to learn content.

Continuing in this application, some wise advice I was given at my first laboratory school training was, "Never assume anything." Your students come with varying degrees of biblical knowledge. Some may be quite familiar with Scripture, with Bible characters and relationships, with customs in biblical times that made perfect sense then. Others, however, may be new to Bible study. All these names, connections, and biblical customs are foreign to them. In order for them to make the brain connections, you must provide a basic framework. If you do not make sure that concepts are understood and connections are made, you will have created some frustrated learners or inadvertently invited some misconnections that lead to misunderstandings. It is well worth a few minutes to make certain that all your students are "on the same page." For some it will be a quick review; for others it will be new and important information. If you want your students' learning to stand on its own, you must provide the initial strong structure. You must make sure the terms and concepts are understandable. Watch your students' faces. You can usually tell when they are lost or confused.

Two relatively simple ways to assure that students are with you is to stop periodically and ask if there are questions or clarifications or to inform your students that they may ask questions any time during the presentation. You will get to know your class members and which options would work better with them.

You may also turn this concept into a creative exercise by explaining a midrash and then having your students create one about the biblical story you are studying. The term *midrash* comes from our Jewish brothers and sisters. It is a story that fills in the blanks of Scripture. A midrash might construct a conversation between Ruth, Orpah, and Naomi or discuss what the lives of Mary and Martha were like after Jesus' ascension or whatever happened to the family of the forgiving father and the prodigal son. A midrash takes nothing away from Scripture; it helps your brain create meaning. I often use this technique in creativity training, and folks really get into it.

Another way for the brain to create meaning is by treating questions as important. If you model this concept by stopping after each new chunk of information and asking if anyone has questions, you are creating an environment where inquiry is an important part of the learning process. You want to make sure students have the information before moving on to the next piece. You do not have to know all the answers. It is perfectly OK to say you do not know and to make suggestions about discovering the answers. Answers may be provided by another student, by referring to a resource book, or by calling on an expert. Answers do not have to be immediate. Suggest Internet sites.

Sometimes it seems it would just be easier if the teacher provided all the answers. This method is potentially harmful in at least three ways: (1) It assumes there is only one right answer. (2) It assumes students do not have the ability to make their own discoveries. (3) It shuts down any further discussion or differing opinions. It effectively shuts down the thinking process of your students since they have no input or personal investment in the answer.

Another aspect of this application is to ask for at least three right answers. Seldom is there only one right answer. The exception of course is talking about factual or statistical information. Looking for several right answers is a much riskier approach to teaching/learning. It is also more brain stimulating and conducive to deeper learning.

Remember, the brain's job is to create meaning. If the right answer is constantly provided, the brain does not have much processing to do and the brain does not have to recall memories of times or events to support or refute the answer.

Yet another way for the brain to create meaning is to use metaphor and simile. These are powerful tools for helping the brain make connections. The Bible is overflowing with these powerful figures of speech. Check the Psalms or The Song of Solomon. Jesus used metaphors and similes to teach God's word. He did this to fulfill what was spoken by the prophets: "I will open my mouth to speak in parables; / I will proclaim what has been hidden from the foundation of the world" (Matthew 13:35).

The power of these figures of speech lies in the fact that they are not meant to be taken literally; rather, they point to a profound meaning beyond the words. The parables are classic examples of metaphor and simile. Jesus used parables constantly to help his listeners understand God's word. The parable of the prodigal son (Luke 15:11-32) has been touted as one of the most powerful metaphors of all time. Just about everyone can relate to one or more of the characters in that story. We can empathize. We understand the feelings of the younger son, the older son, and most important, the message that God, the father, is waiting with open and loving arms for each of us to return. What a blessing! These metaphorical connections engage emotions in a powerful way.

The parable of the laborers in the vineyard (Matthew 20:1-16) is one of the most troubling parables for many people. It makes no sense in our world. Yet, it is not about our world. It is about God's world, God's kingdom; and even our amazing brain needs help with our finite understanding of God's kingdom. This parable and all the parables help us to see what Jesus wanted his listeners then and now to comprehend.

For further consideration, read the Kingdom parables. All the Kingdom parables are an attempt by Jesus to help people understand what God's kingdom is like. Jesus begins the Kingdom parables with the parable of the sower (Matthew 13:1-9). He then goes on to say: The kingdom of God is like

a man who sowed good seed in his field (13:24-30)

a mustard seed (13:31-32)

leaven (13:33)

a treasure hidden in a field (13:44)

a pearl of great value (13:45-46)

a net thrown into the sea (13:47-48)

Most assuredly his listeners could identify with one or more of the comparisons and find some meaning of the kingdom of God. It was (and still is) difficult for the brain to create that kind of meaning. Jesus needed to expand their (and our) thinking. He used things that people understood—farming, fishing, raising grapes, and caring for sheep—to attempt to help people begin to grasp the awesomeness of God's kingdom and God's love.

You can use metaphor and simile in your teaching. A simple way to begin is to ask your students, "Is your faith more like rain or sunshine, an oak or a willow, a door or a window?"

You can create your own combinations by following two rules: (1) Make sure the things you are comparing are compatible (a window or a door, NOT a window or a table); and (2) assure your students there are no right or wrong answers, all answers are acceptable because they reflect how you feel. This can be a powerful and nonthreatening way for students to talk about their faith.

You can use Jesus' "I am" statements as recorded in John's Gospel and ask which of them best describes how your students see Christ. This is a good exercise to do in pairs. It is amazing how much faith is shared when students unpack these statements. You can add another dimension to this lesson by inviting your students to complete ten "I am" statements (literal or metaphorical) about themselves as an advanced organizer. This simple exercise makes the brain work at many levels, as it creates meaning both for Jesus' words and for a deeper glimpse or metaphorical explanation of self.

Try these two simple exercises to help your students understand the concept (and power) of metaphor and simile:

1. Go on a metaphor/simile hunt in the Bible. Choose one or two as a group and explain them.

OR

2. Ask students to individually find their favorite parable and to explain the metaphor or simile. Exercises like this help students use many parts of their brain to create meaning from the parable and to articulate that meaning.

Action Research

How do you help students prepare to learn?

How do you help students remain focused on learning throughout the lesson?

What type of advanced organizers do you/might you use? Be specific.

What type of graphic organizers do you/might you use? Be specific.

How have you captured/might you capture the power of emotions in your class session?

When have you used/might you use metaphor and simile to help students grasp the meaning of a lesson?

Take time to explain the meaning of your favorite parable. How did it feel to think and explain the parable in your own words (to create your meaning)?

Record your students' responses to these various methods of helping the brain create meaning.

Go to page 33. Check to see if there are any references to the brain's need to create meaning in your best or worst list.

Application 3

The brain is sharpened
through problem solving.

Try this experiment: Close your eyes and reflect on a time when your brain recognized a problem with the lesson being presented, perhaps some information that you could not agree to or a phrase that did not make sense. How did you react? You needed to solve that problem to your satisfaction before learning could happen.

My masters degree in creative studies focused on the ability to solve problems. Legend has it that someone once asked Albert Einstein what he would do if he was told the world was coming to an end in sixty minutes. He said that he would spend the first fifty-five minutes discovering what the problem was and the last five minutes solving it. Fascinating. Often we learn much more by defining the problem than from the solution.

Problem solving takes on a multitude of forms. It is something you do all day, every day. Most problems are inconsequential and unconscious. But at least once a day, you may come across a major problem with work, with family, with relationships, with faith. How do you solve problems? Your brain knows.

Your brain solves problems by way of several different procedures:

* Your mind and body cannot be separated. Your body and brain respond automatically to certain stimuli such as touching a hot stove or recoiling at the presence of danger. You do not have any control over that. Your body tells your brain what to do in nanoseconds without your having to think about what you should do.

* Your social brain solves problems by connecting with the brain of another and using his or her skills. In the instance of your car breaking down, you call upon the brain work of the auto mechanic who knows how your car works and who has expertise in that area. Your doctor or financial advisor or pastor fall into this category of solving problems (or preventing them) that you do not have the expertise to do alone.

* Your thinking brain has learned to use materials that extend mem-

ory and that allow you to concentrate on the things that are important to your needs. For instance, sticky notes help you remember dates and to do's, telephone books keep you from having to memorize phone numbers, E-mail address files keep you in contact with friends and clients around the world at a moment's notice. Reference materials either in print or online can provide information at your fingertips.

Multiple Intelligence (MI) Theory is a powerful and useful vehicle in problem solving. I cannot write a text on brain research without returning to the application that changed my life.

My discovery of the work in Multiple Intelligence Theory over a decade ago fits so well into the schema of brain research; indeed this was the link that first tweaked my interest in brain research. If you already know about MI or have read books on the subject (mine are translated for use within the religious community), you may be fascinated at discovering the "why's" that attempt to explain Multiple Intelligence Theory in terms of problem solving. If you are not familiar with Multiple Intelligence Theory or need a more in-depth look, see Resources (page 138).

The essence of Multiple Intelligence Theory is that each person is born with the ability to learn in at least seven different intelligences. (I know some believe in eight or more intelligences. I am a purist. In all my research and experience, the seven core intelligences are the ones that can be proved and identified by participants—my own action research. I am open to new findings and will continue to follow the writings in this area. The bottom line of this theory is there are many ways to learn.)

In the context of this book, I would like to explore MI from a different slant and focus on the premise that the brain is sharpened through problem solving. Much of the brain's effort is put into solving problems—varying in intensity from What shall I wear today? to How will I find time in my busy schedule to be engaged in Bible study? to What ways can I help my teenage son stay out of the drug scene? You are engaged in hundreds of areas of problem solving each day. Many of these details are handled automatically by your brain without you having to deal with the decisions. More about this in a later application. For now, let us propose that you need to solve a problem. Your brain solves problems in many and varied ways. To bring this concept to your classroom, I would like to focus on Multiple Intelligence Theory as a problem-solving technique you can use in your lessons.

Each of the seven core intelligences falls into one of the three areas of problem solving that our species needs to deal with. These major problem-solving areas are the temporal, spatial, and social elements of our daily need to deal with others and self. I will break the intelligences down into their brain specific problem-solving areas as defined by brain researcher and educator Robert Sylwester.

The first categories of intelligence require the brain to process and communicate temporal and sequential information. These areas of problem solving deal with the processing of information, analysis of the information, and the cause-and-effect factors involved with the information. The intelligences that fall into this category are Verbal/Linguistic (V/L), Musical/Rhythmic (M/R), and Logical /Mathematical (L/M).

Verbal/Linguistic: the use of reading, writing, speaking, and listening in helping students learn. The ability to speak a language forms long before any language is spoken. Children are born with brain connections to speak any of the world's three thousand plus known languages. The language they eventually speak is the one spoken in the child's individual environment. When not put into use, the neurons for the other languages die off from lack of use (not to worry, you have many billions more). Spoken language develops before the brain begins to encode any written words. For families this means it is critical to talk to infants and children; you are sparking dendrites and encouraging brain strength. Children of lower income, lower educated families hear approximately five thousand words in the first two years. Children of upper income and higher educated families hear approximately twenty thousand words in the first two years. This is a critical factor in later learning. All the words a child hears, even though the words are not comprehended, establish neural connections that can be activated later.

The brain interprets language in two essential areas: the linking of language and thought occur in Wernicke's Area, in the temporal lobes; and grammatical structure and word production occur in Broca's Area in the frontal lobes. When the brain makes the connection between these two areas, children begin to speak in sentences. As you develop in your faith, stories begin to take shape that connect your understanding of God's world through your experiences.

Words are important. They help us define our spiritual questions, doubts, fears, witnessing, and celebrating. If we could not process our thoughts into words, we could not communicate our feelings and needs.

One of the ways we know about God is through words. Some believe the Bible is the inerrant word of God. Others believe the Bible is the inspired word of God. Still others believe the Bible records God's message to the people for whom it was intended, with all the cultural nuances and mores of the time. It then becomes your job to help students articulate their understandings and beliefs of what Scripture is saying to them today.

Words help your students solve problems with understanding Scripture. Consider the Creation story in Genesis. An entire lesson can focus on Adam and Eve's expulsion from the garden. Was their act of eating the fruit disobedience, hubris (excessive pride, self-confidence, arrogance), the beginning of consciousness, or listening to an authority (the serpent) other than God? Words have power to expand Scripture, without diminishing it.

Another way to connect brain research to your classroom is to encourage the use of words through storytelling in at least two ways: (1) tell the biblical story and (2) invite your students to tell their own faith stories. Then encourage your students to connect the two and make their own discoveries. Students will have to link their language and thought processes and then put together the words to tell their story. Two lobes of the brain come into play and continue to be strengthened.

Storytelling is a powerful tool to help students of all ages make these connections. Words connect us to one another and to concepts. Good storytellers use words as literary tools to evoke emotions. When you encourage students to tell their faith stories, they must use various parts of their brain to connect the words in sequence. Stories have the ability to communicate an event through the filters of personal experience and emotion. Connecting V/L intelligence and brain research helps imprint the story on the brain.

Telling personal stories becomes a powerful problem-solving technique when you take time to listen. I am a good listener. I am not the keeper of the answers; but I have discovered, after years of people asking if I have time to talk, that simply listening to people tell their story is therapeutic and cathartic. Telling the story serves as a problem-solving technique for the teller.

Part B of storytelling is equally important: listening. Problematically, many students in any grade in school or beyond school have been taught very little about listening. Listening is a skill as well as a problem-solving technique. There are books related to listening skills. That is not the purpose of this book. For purposes of your classroom situation, you might help students listen by breaking them into pairs and setting a timer. One person is speaker, one is listener, and then they get to switch places. Not a big deal, except only one person can speak. The listener's job is to listen and not to interrupt in any way until the timer goes off. Then the listener reflects back what he or she heard the speaker saying. It may feel contrived at first; but once they get the hang of listening without interrupting and providing feedback, you can eliminate the timer. You might ask how it feels to really focus on listening or to be really listened to and bring the point home. The brain works harder when it is assigned to really listen.

Similarly, when using a video or reading a biblical story, ask students questions in advance (AO) to help them listen and focus on the content. This focus causes the brain to pay more attention, to solve the problem of the question you pose. Listening for pertinent information is critical to complete learning and problem solving.

In training I use a fictional case study about two scientists who both need the same commodity to solve a major world problem. A greater problem is there is a limited quantity of the item available. When students are paired up and each takes the role of one of the scientists, the problem can be solved easily IF they really listen to what the other is saying. Many problems in churches and church school classes occur because people do not really listen to one another. You will be doing a great service to your students and their brains if you help them develop listening skills as part of the V/L intelligence.

Another area critical to V/L learning is that you are living in a time when you cannot make assumptions that people know what you are talking about. It is critical to help students define words, discover relationships, understand doctrine or even what a particular denomination's stance is on major issues. You must not assume that your students know Scripture, prayers, or creeds. Use the written word. Set an example of finding Scripture by referring to the table of contents to find a book in the Bible. List vocabulary words that may be foreign, and ask if anyone has words to add to your list. Help the brain solve problems; do not create them by assumption of information. Small problems become major brain stumbling blocks when there is lack of information or misinformation.

Yet another critical area of V/L learning and problem solving is not putting students on the spot for any reason. I seldom use absolutes; but I'm going to now—NEVER simply ask someone to read aloud, at any age. Some children, youth, or adults have minimal reading skills. It will be embarrassing. Remember the brain shuts down when it feels threatened. It is much more brain safe to ask volunteers to read.

The next intelligence included in this first trio of problem-solving techniques the brain employs is *Musical/Rhythmic:* the use of music in all its forms, rhythms, pitches, and timbres to enhance learning.

Music provides emotional content through all its components. Often you must find ways to communicate beyond the written or spoken word. Sometimes the words of a song are the trigger to our hearts; other times it is the music itself that causes us to feel joy or sadness. Each student in your class of five or twenty or fifty students hearing the same piece of music may have different reactions due to his or her own experiences. How many of us are emotionally stirred by Handel's "Messiah" or Judy Collins's rendition of "Amazing Grace" or a joyful expression of "Shout to the Lord"? Music has the power to take us places words alone cannot.

Music is the first intelligence formed, a precursor to spoken language. It is arguably the most powerful intelligence. The brain seems to learn most thoroughly through the M/R intelligence. Think about it. Test this statement with your own reality. Can you sing words to a song you haven't heard in years? Do you hum the "ABC Song" when you look up a word in the dictionary? Your brain stores music in many different areas, making recall more accessible.

Many people, when they are in a spiritual crisis or when large problems seem overwhelming, cannot find words to express their feelings. Often they turn to music to calm their souls. Hearing music from your childhood or from a high or low point in your life can return your brain instantly to that time. Alzheimer patients who have not spoken a coherent word for years can sing songs of their youth and dance to songs that return them to a better time.

A moving story about music and problem solving concerns a young woman in a seminary class. Her professor was singing "I Come to the Garden" in a less than sacred way. She approached him after class and told him she was offended at his treatment of that song. She had been sexually abused by her father for years before she was old enough to get out of the situation. She said she sang that song daily to keep her sanity. Music is powerful and sometimes life saving.

On a lighter note, when you need to solve a problem or to learn a specific set of information, sing it. A woman in one of my adult laboratory school settings was excited about sharing a story. She is a high school physics teacher and struggles with ways to help her students learn the formulae necessary to understand the concepts of physics. She taught her students the formulas translated to music. During a test, she would often hear humming; but the students did very well on the tests. Even years later, if she met one of her students, the student would inevitably sing a formula. She helped students learn formulae to music intuitively and was delighted to know there was research that supported her technique.

I can teach any Scripture passage to the tune of "Jesus Loves Me." When you sing Scripture, you tell the story in several ways: words, rhythm, pitch, tone, and sometimes volume.

To connect brain research to your classroom, use music to enhance learning. Students can speak of their life and faith stories through music when they cannot do it otherwise. Use music too as an advanced organizer to set up your lesson or as a form of prayer or as a study of how Scripture was presented throughout the centuries. Many of the psalms appear in our hymns. Psalmists were the musicians of their time. David and other creators of the psalms poured out their emotions in the psalms—everything from joy to heartbreak is reflected in the psalms. Use them. Music evokes emotion, and emotion promotes complex learning. Go on a Scripture/song hunt. Find Scripture verses that have been put to music, or begin with the hymnal and discover songs that have their origin in Scripture.

The third intelligence in this problem-solving sequence is *Logical/Mathematical:* the use of cognitive functions such as sequencing, problem solving, performing mathematical tasks in learning. L/M intelligence is a necessary part of our cognitive functions. Children begin to learn to put things in order and to count at a relatively early age. This is an important developmental stage. Children also learn at an early age about cause and effect. Crying brings someone to help. Dropping a toy means someone picks it up and returns it. Playing peek-a-boo is much more than a game to a young child. A child discovers that when someone disappears, he or she will come back. This is how babies learn. This is how they discover their world is safe and predictable. Patterning and sequencing, cause and effect, are skills begun as babies and continued throughout learning. It is how you figure things out and how you solve problems of all magnitude.

L/M provides the kind of precise intellectual functioning that makes buildings and bridges stand ("close enough" does not do it). Many computer games are based on discovering patterns and sequences and acting on them. L/M intelligence is so broad, with so many sub skills, it can be observed in both brain hemispheres, particularly in the frontal lobes.

To connect this brain research to your classroom, provide a way to use order and sequence in the lesson. One thing needs to follow another in a logical way in order for it to make sense to a percentage of your students. Students who prefer this intelligence like to know how, why, where, and when things took place when studying Scripture. Spiritual hungers are sometimes fed by facts. The story without these supporting facts does not help them understand. Their brains need this information to make learning complete. Use graphic organizers either individually or as a class to present in a visual format the sequence of the story. Provide parts of the story and let students put them in the correct order. With children and teens (and some adults) you can create games based on order and sequence to sharpen this intelligence.

These are the students who will struggle with questions and issues and not be completely satisfied with clichés such as, "You just need to believe." They want to know why Jesus was rejected by his community and how he appeared to his followers in the upper room after his resurrection. Often you do not have direct answers. Do not try to fake it. Simply say you do not have all the answers, and refer them to further scholarly materials. To some questions there are no direct answers. Metaphor or simile sometimes works in these cases. I tell my students, "I don't have a clue as to how E-mail works. All I know is, I can type words into my computer and a friend in California, in Kentucky, or in Denmark will receive them in seconds. I don't understand. I only know it works."

It is not difficult to hook into deeper learning for these folks. Provide resources or Web sites for them to solve their problems by making their own discoveries, and they are happy. During adult Bible study, these are the people who willingly do the digging to provide background information. To some these details seem like extraneous bits of information. To the L/M learner, they are required for learning to be complete.

The next category of problem-solving intelligences deals with space and place or the ability to understand the concept of your place and how you deal with the space around you.

Visual/Spatial: the necessity of forming a visual picture of something in order for the most complete learning to occur and to determine how you fit into your environment. We know that the left hemisphere of the brain processes verbal descriptions and directions, while the right hemisphere processes visual components of a map, pictures, videos, and so on. Provide your students' brains with both kinds of information. To help meet your V/S problem-solving needs, I have specifically asked for graphics of brain components to be added to this book. Some of you need to visualize aspects of the brain to help you "see" what I'm talking about. Your brain will better be able to understand neurons, axons, dendrites, and an overall view of the brain if they are presented both graphically and linguistically. (See pages 28–31.)

You can ask your students to close their eyes and "see" in their mind's eye a picture of what you are discussing. V/S students can do this task. They can place themselves at the Sea of Galilee with sun sparkling on the water and the fishing boats dotting the horizon. They can transform themselves into a specific place and visualize their surroundings. It is not necessary to have actually been at the Sea of Galilee to accomplish this task; the brain can call up an image of a body of water and go from there. It helps to plug into the story when students can visualize a setting and place themselves in that setting.

Some students cannot do this at all. Their brains do not function easily in this task. Tell your students up front that not everyone's brain is wired to do this, and that is OK. Invite them simply to relax and listen to the words of the story.

To connect this brain research to your classroom for V/S students of all ages, mental images of the scriptural setting, pictures, or graphics are essential. Maps, slides, videos, objects, costumes, graphs are all visual enhancers and will add to students' deeper understanding of what is being taught. The brain processes visual stimuli in several different ways, and each way adds to the imprinting of learning. (See Application 8, page 104.)

Another way for your brain to connect visually is to find Scripture in the *Good News Bible*. Annie Vallotton's drawings bring Scripture to life. Often she can express feelings with a few strokes of a pen that words alone cannot capture.

Body/Kinesthetic: the use of body to move and manipulate to enhance learning through developing changes in muscle control and body memory.

It takes several areas of your brain to accomplish simple movements. Much of your daily movement falls into the category of procedural memories. You do not have to think about how to walk, climb stairs, or run for a bus. Your procedural memory is already programmed to accomplish those tasks. But there are other ways movement is involved in problem solving. Nearly half of your brain cells are located in the cerebellum (little brain located at the back of the brain). The main job of the cerebellum is to deal with movement. Whenever you move, the cerebellum becomes involved; and since that is where most of your brain cells are located, it simply makes sense that movement and learning are connected. Also involved in B/K intelligence are the limbic system, which triggers emotions for movement, and the motor cortex, which codes movements.

To help understand the problem of how David killed Goliath with a sling and a stone, you can create a sling like the one David might have used. Take a six-by-four-inch scrap of fabric and gather it at each lengthwise end, securing it with a needle and thread. Find two pieces of heavy twine, and tie one to each end of the fabric pouch. You have a sling. Explain that the stone was placed into the pouch and swung around the head until momentum was established. The sling was then aimed at the object and the stone traveled at a great speed toward its target. Physically using the sling (in an open area) will imprint this story and the problem solving on the brain. This is only one example of how to incorporate B/K learning into solving problems in your lesson.

A more practical connection of this brain research to your classroom is to remember that the brain needs movement to remain alert and engaged. Movement encourages blood flow, which provides oxygen to the brain. People who learn best through this intelligence need to move. They may pace to enhance thinking, or they may manipulate an object. Their tactile senses need to be included to complete their learning.

Students of any age will benefit when they are encouraged to act out a story. When a student takes on a role and moves in response to that role, his or her entire body becomes involved in the act of learning. Getting physically involved promotes learning by hooking into various areas of the brain. Actually, it does not even have to be that involved. Children love to, need to, move. Get them moving around the room in games or roleplaying.

Some adult students are more reluctant to move. It has to do with safety, not so much a literal (although it may be literal) concern for safety as a psychological sense of "looking good" or not appearing foolish in front of your peers. Many adults find this the most difficult intelligence to incorporate. How do you handle this? One right answer is, you can move. If you change your place in the room, students will follow you either with their eyes or by turning their whole body. Other right answers are that you may ask them to turn and face a partner or to move on a continuum or simply stand up to think. The key is to get them to move. (See the discussion on brain breaks, page 130.)

The last category to be considered is problem solving in your personal intelligences: intrapersonal and interpersonal. Both of these intelligences function much of the time without your conscious awareness. You don't have to think about talking with others about a problem or about thinking a problem through by yourself.

Intrapersonal: the use of inner resources, reflection, and pulling information from within. This intelligence is based largely on your values and is located in the limbic system, the seat of our emotions. This intelligence is one of the last to take on an advanced form as it requires a vast bank of experiences to draw from. It also requires a maturation of the frontal lobe, which happens in adolescence.

To integrate this brain research into your classroom make certain to incorporate time to reflect and absorb the learning that is taking place. If you get nothing else from this book, incorporating this information on reflection time will make a significant change in your students' learning. I will discuss this as a separate application.

The Intrapersonal learner needs time to process information for it to make sense.

The other personal intelligence is *Interpersonal*: the social intelligence. You are a social being; you need to learn to read others and to react on that information to function in your world.

Children primarily learn their social intelligence, how to function with others, in the home environment. They have to expand on this learning with peers when they begin formal education. Social learning is not an automatic response. Young children (and some not so young) are self-centered. They see the world functioning around them and for their needs. They need to be taught to share, to take turns, to wait until someone else is finished speaking. All these may seem like simple problems to solve, but ask any preschool teacher and you will discover they take skill building.

As you progress into youth and adulthood, you expand your social learning by discovering how to read body language and other physical reactions. You learn to learn from others and to work together to solve problems and to complete tasks.

To integrate this brain research into your classroom, be certain to incorporate both small and large group discussion. Allow time for students to work together in small groups for cooperative learning. They will sharpen their skills for dealing with others in a social and learning situation. When you learn from one another, by speaking and by listening, you become more deeply involved in your own learning and faith growth. You learn when you witness to your own faith journey and when you listen to the stories of faith shared by your group.

DISCIPLE BIBLE STUDY is a prime example of the combining of the personal intelligences. Year after year, my students say that it is the best of both worlds. The reading and research is a necessary component to allow time to think about the story and to weigh it against what they know and against their values. When they come together to talk about their reading, to ask questions, to raise doubts, and to clarify misunderstandings—all done in an atmosphere of love and acceptance—true learning takes place.

Interpersonal skills include being able to deal with other people. A great exercise to practice these skills is to form students into equal groups (numbers will depend on class size) with at least three students per group. Give each group a sheet of paper. Assign a task that includes coming to a group consensus. For example, you might assign the Ten Commandments and have each group record them in an order that would make the most sense in today's world. The group must all agree on the order. Give them seven minutes and eleven seconds to complete this task. Have each group present its completed list to the whole class. Debrief the experience on a spiritual level of what is most important to them and on an Interpersonal skill level: How did it feel to have your ideas accepted or rejected? Were you willing to sacrifice your thoughts to go along with the group and arrive at consensus? Debriefing is a powerful learning tool.

Another way to hone your Interpersonal skills is to use Polarity Management. This is a tool that forces students to interact and to look at all sides of an issue. Choose a topic that has some controversy, as, the church should be inclusive (everyone is invited to come) or exclusive (anyone can attend; but, if you want to be a full member, you must attend worship regularly, engage in Bible study, serve in some capacity, pray daily, and tithe). Prepare four sheets of paper. One says INCLUSIVE +'s, one is labeled INCLUSIVE -'s, one is labeled EXCLUSIVE +'s and the last one EXCLUSIVE -'s. Place each sheet in a different corner of the room.

Form your students into four equal groups. Have each group select a recorder. Assign groups at random to each sheet of paper. Tell them that they have four minutes and thirty-six seconds to write ONLY comments that are applicable for their sheet of paper (such as, INCLUSIVE +). Tell them they do not have to believe in this stance, they simply must recognize and record all the pluses for an INCLUSIVE church. Assure them that each group will have an opportunity to discuss and record applications for each polarity. At the end of the specified time, blow a whistle or give them some clue to move in a clockwise rotation to the next sheet of paper. The same rules apply. Follow this procedure until each group has had an opportunity to explore each polarity.

Debrief this exercise by pulling the group together and asking, "How did it feel to be forced to come up with reasons to support something you do not necessarily believe in? How did it feel to have to listen to someone's views that were different from yours? How did it feel to get your beliefs on paper?"

A final word on MI and the brain: Your students are a living, working combination of all their genetic makeup as well as of their life experience. Adults have more experience to draw on than youth or children, but all have the ability to use the brain's problem-solving skills. Children and youth are taught problem solving from elementary school through high school. Educators know the skills involved help keep the brain sharp. Adults may or may not have been taught to hone these skills. Use a biblical story as a base, and ask questions that cause the brain to work harder in any of the ways mentioned above.

Accept the different ways your students learn. Recognize each is created by God and is to be honored in the learning place. Be sure to include a variety of intelligences in your lessons. Even if you primarily use the lecture method, you can give students objects to focus on while you speak. You can use visuals to strengthen your point. You can take reflection breaks by asking students to turn to a neighbor and to talk about what the lesson means to them personally or what their own experience says about this story. The brain is unique. Be sure to honor diversity.

Action Research

Invite your students to list the "problem solving" tasks they have done that day.

How do you practice problem-solving techniques in your lessons?

How might you incorporate problem solving as you plan your lessons?

Consider your own problem-solving techniques. Which intelligences do you rely on most to solve problems?

Check page 33 to see if any of the problem-solving issues appear on your best/worst learning list.

Application 4

The brain is uniquely organized with differences of learning preference.

Try this exercise: Close your eyes and recall a time when you just "got it" in a learning situation. What were the circumstances? Do you learn most completely through pictures or words? What does your personality type have to do with the way you learn? Each person has preferred ways of knowing. You can learn in any number of ways, but you have ways that make learning easier.

Since this is a resource about the brain, let's begin this application with a further look at split-brain, brain dominant, brain laterality information. Many (not all) researchers discredit any mention of brain-dominant significance in terms of education; but for some reason, among educators the theory will not go away. Perhaps educators have significant insight into the action research that supports what they know of this theory. Another explanation is that the brain-dominant theory is a simplistic (if not totally accurate) way of helping students understand that people learn differently. Most students can tell you if they believe they are more left brained or right brained. Try it. Ask your students. Brain-dominant theory has been part of our cultural language since the 1970's, and people can identify with it.

Very few researchers or educators will find fault with the bottom line, which is that you need to address both hemispheres of the brain for the most complete learning to take place.

For over thirty years, to a lesser or greater degree, emphasis has been placed on the functions of each hemisphere. The left hemisphere, which controls the right side of the body, is the logical and rational area that is primarily involved with the more cognitive functions of reading, writing, speaking, problem solving, and the like. This left hemisphere is the more analytical, factual, and evaluative hemisphere. It wants to know how the parts fit together before it can create the whole piece of information. The left hemisphere is responsible for the literal interpretation of words. It processes information according to all the above qualities. The left hemisphere loves to make sense of time and sequence.

For your purposes, Bible study students who favor their left hemisphere will want to know the distance and to locate on a (topographical) map the exact journey of the traveler who was helped by the good Samaritan. They will find a lesson incomplete that does not contain some statistics or factual information. They might ask, "How do you know this is true?"

FYI: The left hemisphere does not deal well with metaphor or visualization. These students prefer more concrete examples. They often see metaphor and visualization exercises as irrelevant and become frustrated. They want to cut right to the chase and get into the lesson.

I have a dear friend who is learning to use metaphors. She has always been involved in the world of finances and is a methodical, process-oriented, and structured thinker. To her delight one day she made a statement; and with an impish grin asked, "Was that a metaphor?" She is training herself to allow the power of metaphor to enter her world and expand her thinking.

The right hemisphere, which controls the left side of the body, is more creative and intuitive. It gathers information from images rather than words and can track spatial reasoning. The right hemisphere is charged with recognizing faces and places. The right hemisphere deals with a holistic view, needing to see the whole picture before it can fit the parts in place.

For your purposes, Bible study students who favor their right hemisphere will deal more readily with the images of people crossing to the other side of a road and a man being hoisted onto a donkey to be carried somewhere to be cared for. These students do not really care about distances and locations. They are interested in the concept of caring for the injured man and the metaphorical connection to our present lives.

FYI: The right hemisphere does not depend on statistical information to get the picture. Right-brain students may find this kind of detail irrelevant and unnecessary to their holistic understanding of the biblical story.

What is an educator to do? Do you go with scientific brain researchers who claim that none of this makes any sense in a research setting? Do you go with the action research of your experience? Do you dismiss the whole thing as unimportant? I believe jargon and semantics may be getting in the way of helping you understand the differences in learning needs. Let's try a semantic-free approach based on what we do know about how the brain is uniquely organized with differences of talents and preferences.

We do know that

* there are differences in the ways students learn;

* the brain hemispheres are connected, and information is constantly flowing in each direction faster than the speed of light;

* the processing of parts and wholes always interact and information is dealt with simultaneously in both hemispheres;

* the functioning of the brain is so complex that to attempt to assign a single task to imprinting information seems absurd, as "That is a right-brained task";

* since the brain is uniquely organized, educators must incorporate diverse and varied techniques and processes when creating a plan for teaching/learning.

An update of similar analysis of the functions of the two hemispheres is presented for your consideration. Two independent but interactive ways of your brain processing information are perhaps a more current way of approaching the differences in the functions of each hemisphere. Seymour Epstein has labeled the two interactive functions as Experiential and Rational. Briefly stated

Experiential Processing includes but is not limited to the following defining characteristics: interpersonal, emotionally engaging, story-telling, perceptual, positive, imaginative, able to be flexible.

Learning strategies most often associated with this method of processing are emotions, moods, stories, senses, pictures, metaphors, action movement, and images.

Rational Processing includes but is not limited to the following defining characteristics: analytical, conscious, formal, abstract, organized, conceptual.

Learning strategies most often associated with this method of processing are charts, tables, graphs, and systems analysis.

Relating to the bottom line of brain lateral theory—make sure you incorporate learning strategies from both hemispheres in your teaching/learning plans. Those who favor one hemisphere or the other will still benefit from the inclusion of strategies for both.

Let me offer some suggestions for inclusion of both strategies: when you lecture, include stories or examples; when you do an exercise, take time to debrief it; when you read something, provide a way to experience it; when you have been intense, lighten up (I use cartoons).

Same subject, different approach. Each of you is wonderfully and fearfully made by God. Each of you is unique and different; there is only one of YOU. In the past educators tended to teach as if everyone was the same, with the same learning needs and wants. Everyone was on the same page at the same time. We know differently now.

Any good educator has intuitively known this basic concept for years: Students learn differently. An attempt to act on this concept was the "Learning Center" approach, made popular in the experiential age of the 1970's and 1980's. Different areas of a room would be set up with activities to help students experience a lesson through crafts, art, music, or reading/writing. Learning centers helped in an effort to allow students to experience alternative ways of approaching a subject.

Curriculums are now available based on an ancient/future approach of combining what was tried and tested through learning centers and the newer brain-related approach of Multiple Intelligence Theory. This ancient/future approach to teaching Sunday school began in the late 1980's in a suburb of Chicago and is most widely known as "The Workshop Rotation Model." Since then, many people have seen the advantages of this model and have adapted it to their specific needs.

Essentially a workshop rotation model provides an in-depth study of Scripture, as opposed to most curriculum that provides a breadth approach. In essence rotation curriculum will focus on one biblical story for four to eight weeks. Each week students experience the story presented (often by a person gifted in that area) in a different way—through music, art, drama, games, storytelling, food preparation, science, and videos or computers. Not all churches use all eight weeks. Most use a four-week rotation. This ancient/future concept of teaching the biblical story provides for learning in all the intelligences and insures diversity in the teaching/learning process.

More diversity emerges in the form of personalities. We each have one. Your class will be a collection of many different personalities. They will surface and, unless you deal effectively with them, they may disrupt your class. Personalities enter into teaching/learning by way of group dynamics. There are many types of personality inventories available both in the religious and in the secular world. I am most conversant with the MBTI®—the Myers-Briggs Type Inventory®. I am an MBTI® trainer and have used this instrument for years in both religious and secular settings. Essentially, you behave in certain identifiable ways because of the way your brain is wired. In a thumbnail explanation you score somewhere on a continuum between two categories in four distinct areas: You either lean toward Extroversion or Introversion, Sensing or Intuition, Thinking or Feeling, and Judging or Perceiving. Remember, you fall somewhere on the continuum. Each person has a profile consisting of one of each pair of the categories, signified by an initial. Each person is either E or I, S or N, F or T, J or P. The four letters are a code for the person's profile. Mine is ENFJ. Statistically, people fall into a normal bell curve, with the fewest numbers falling at either extreme. A brief explanation and some ideas for dealing with these personalities in your classroom follow.

The first category deals with where you get your energy from and where to focus your attention: Extrovert or Introvert.

Extroverts get their energy from the outside world. They love to be with people and learn best in situations where they can talk with and learn from others. Small and/or large group discussion is a key factor in their learning needs. They learn best when they are involved in a conversation and are able to test their ideas with those of others.

FYI: Extroverts may talk too much and dominate a discussion. Extroverts are the students who will often speak without taking time to think things through. A way to deal positively with extroverts is to form dyads or pairs. Tell them they will have two minutes each to talk about your topic. At the end of two minutes ring a bell or blow a whistle or give some strong signal that it is time for the other person to talk. A talking stick is another way to manage persons dominating conversation. Sit in a circle. Open a topic. The only person allowed to speak is the one holding the talking stick, which is in the center of the circle. When someone has something to contribute to the topic at hand, he or she walks to the center of the circle, picks up the stick, may speak for two minutes, and then must replace the stick in the center of the circle.

Introverts get their energy from going within. They learn best in situations that allow for reflection and for think time. They do not speak often; but when they do speak, they usually have something important to say. Both methods listed above work for introverts too. Dyads allow introverts to speak in a less threatening setting (remember, the brain does not function well under stress). Often introverts will feel more comfortable speaking to one other person rather than in front of the whole group. The talking stick allows introverts the think time they need. They will seldom be the first people to take the stick; but after considerable time to think, they will often have some profound words to share with the group.

FYI: These are the students who usually do not speak out in class. Extroverts jump right in, and introverts never have an opportunity to speak. You, as facilitator, can require "think time" by setting a timer or watching the second hand of a clock. No one is allowed to speak for sixty-two seconds. This is a valuable lesson for all students.

The second category is how you gather information: Sensing or Intuition.

Sensors get their information through their five senses: How much does it weigh? How big is it? What does it taste or smell like? We know that the brain is in its best learning mode when all senses are used. For your students to learn most concretely and fully, include things in your lesson to see, hear, taste, touch, and smell. This is an easy and rewarding task for you as facilitator to encourage. You do not have to provide everything yourself. Let someone who likes to bake bring in a food likely to have been served in biblical times. This will often include at least four of your senses. Play music that involves the brain in the mood you want to create. Visuals have already been mentioned as a necessary tool for the brain. Involve as many senses as you can for more complete learning.

FYI: The sensing types need to have sensory input presented as factual information. For them learning is not complete without this information.

As facilitator, you can provide resource materials including Web sites for further research or be certain to obtain factual information about your lesson and have it readily available for your students. You can make certain that sensory information is included in each lesson.

Intuitors get their information from their sixth sense or "gut feeling." The intuitor's mantra is, "I know what I know, don't confuse me with the facts." Your students who are strong at intuiting like to take a stab at what might have happened and why. They need to see the big picture and then fit the details in. They are experts at seeing possibilities and value imagination and creativity. They love the "what if?" questions.

FYI: Intuitors like to see the whole picture. They must get a sense of what you are doing and why you are doing it in order to make sense of the details. As facilitator, you can provide an outline of the lesson so intuitors can see where the lesson is going. Their brains will then focus on the pieces and parts that make up the whole.

The third category is how you make decisions: Thinking or Feeling.

Thinking types make decisions with their heads. They live in a logical, sequential, and cognitive world. They make decisions objectively by looking at cause and effect, by analyzing and weighing the evidence. They want objective standards for truth.

FYI: These students' brains need time and information to analyze a lesson. If it does not make sense to them, their brain cannot grasp the significance. Often they have trouble with a Scripture because it does not make sense. How could Jesus appear in a room that was locked? As facilitator, you can ask for their help in setting up a sequence of events and cause and effect relationships. These students enjoy working with problems.

Feeling types make decisions with their hearts. They want to do what feels good and makes people comfortable. They avoid conflict. They have strong person-centered values. These are the students who are sympathetic, understanding, and appreciative.

FYI: Feelers may become annoyed with thinkers and vice versa. They do not understand what makes the other tick. Why can't you just accept the story? Why does it have to make sense in a cognitive way? As facilitator, you need to reiterate that each brain is wired a bit differently; and this wiring enables us to learn in different ways. One way is not better or worse than the other, just different. Encourage students who differ to learn from one another.

Just a note: Feeling types DO think and thinking types DO feel. It is their decision-making process that is involved here.

The last category is how you orient yourself to the outside world: Judging or Perceiving.

Judging types like their world to be orderly and planned. They like to be in control of the situation. They like structure and like to bring closure before moving on.

FYI: These students function best when they can sense order and structure. Their brains will not be able to focus if they sense chaos. They must make order out of the chaos before they can learn. They like to control their environment. They prefer a direct route. As facilitator, you can create order by posting an agenda, by telling them ahead of time what is expected, and by following a certain structure.

Perceiving types thrive by being allowed to be flexible and spontaneous. They like to keep their options open and are always willing to try something new. They live in and enjoy the moment and can adapt to new experiences readily.

FYI: These students have a problem bringing closure to anything. They always want to see what else is out there. They may appear to be disorganized: not true. They are organized in a different way. They prefer to take the scenic route but eventually arrive at their destination. As facilitator, you can be open to a teachable moment and go with it.

Find out if there is anyone in your church who is MBTI® certified. If there is someone who is willing to come to your class and provide more extensive information, it will help you and your students understand the class diversity.

By involving your students in assessment and understanding of their own diversity, you will help them acknowledge and become comfortable with what other students need to make learning complete. Once you come to understand what the brain needs, you can adapt the learning situation, accept diversity, and foster greater learning.

Something else to consider: Your personality type often (unconsciously) dictates your teaching style. My ENFJ personality usually makes my classroom energetic, talkative, imaginative, and caring; and I ALWAYS have a lesson plan. I remind myself to make sure I allow think time and quiet time, that I include facts, provide for logical thinking processes, and put the lesson plan away to go with an exciting flow of the class. Understanding how you function lets you adjust for the reality of your situation.

To integrate brain research into your classroom, remember the bottom line message here is that each brain is wired just a bit differently with different needs to make learning happen. There is no right or wrong way to learn. Once you are aware of the learning needs of your students, you can adjust your teaching/learning style to meet those needs.

Other studies explain diversity. There are books specifically dedicated to that kind of information. For the purposes of this brain book, suffice it to say that your students are diverse in the way they learn and behave. As facilitator, you need to be aware of this and to make your teaching/learning setting as amiable to the brain's uniqueness as possible. You cannot be all things to all people and accommodate everyone's needs, but you can point out diversity and encourage the acceptance of differences and the blessings that come from sharing diverse views. If people believe they are accepted for who they are, they will find their own ways to meet their learning needs. Accepting differences is the key.

The spiritual aspects of your students have differences as well. Some will need to pray aloud; some want silent prayer. Some of your students may be into social justice and need to support/become involved with a mission project while others are into laying on of hands. To some only the King James Version of Scripture is acceptable while others are excited about *The Message*.

Some of your students are "seekers," with little background but a deep hunger to know God's Word. To some of them singing two-hundred-year-old songs and traditional liturgy have no relevance to today's cyber world. Some have grown up in the church and are filled with the tradition and see the church as their only point of stability in a rapidly changing world.

The church is struggling with these diversity issues constantly. One of the right answers is CHOICES. Many churches offer different styles of worship either concurrently or at different times or even days of the week. By offering choices, they can meet the worship and learning needs of the diverse community. Many churches also offer choices for religious education. No longer is Sunday morning the only or the best time to offer Bible study.

One last brief comment on the diversity of the brain (there are whole books on this subject) is that male and female brains are different (no surprise here). Prenatal development of male and female brains differs in slight but educationally profound ways. Male brains are roughly fifteen percent larger than female brains (remember it is not the size of the brain that matters but how it is used). The cerebral cortex is thicker on the right hemisphere for males and on the left for females. This supports research that states males tend to be more visually oriented (they look at maps) and females are more verbal (we ask for directions).

When dealing with abstract problems, males tap into the right hemisphere while females are more adept at communicating between both hemispheres. The corpus callosum is thicker in females.

Your brain seeks to create meaning. You must offer choices to meet those needs, either in one setting or many settings and times.

Action Research

List as many of the various diversities you can think of in your classroom.

How might you make discoveries about these diversities?

How do you honor your students' preferences for learning?

How do you honor your students' personality differences?

Check page 33 to see if any of the information presented appears in your best/worst learning experience list.

Application 5

The brain thrives
in an enriched environment.

Try this exercise: Close your eyes and recall a time when you were in an environment that was enriched. Picture this environment in your mind's eye. Recall the sights, sounds, smells, textures, and maybe even tastes. Think of how this environment helped you learn.

Your brain creates itself according to your needs all your life. It is such an amazing organism that it can change and recreate itself in response to your environment, your lifestyle, or physical changes due to injury or disease.

In some circles it was thought your brain was "hard wired," and beyond a certain point it could not develop or change. We know this is not true. The challenge remains: Is there a specific time the brain appears to be more open to learning, a window of opportunity? Neuroscientists disagree. Some believe the critical time for learning is pre-birth to age four; others say to age ten; still others believe important learning takes place after age ten when the dendrite pruning process seems to be over, when your brain has shed those unneeded connections. Other neuroscientists believe, as do I, that the brain never stops learning. There may be more opportune times when the brain is most ready to learn a foreign language or to learn music. This does not mean you cannot learn these things at any stage of life, it simply means that particular learning seems to happen more readily at certain times. We now know that learning does not happen in rigid stages. Like a spiral, there are opportune times to learn and there are opportunities to learn again.

The long-standing battle over which is more important, nurture or nature, seems irrelevant the more we know about the brain. BOTH are critical to the formation and continuation of brain power. Children born to health-conscious, caring parents grow in an environment rich with physical, emotional, and mental stimulation. Children born to parents on drugs or alcohol, for instance, often grow up in devastating, unhealthy, and emotionally impoverished environments. Yet, these children can overcome obstacles; they can and do learn. It is a challenge to educators to make learning relevant and readily available for them. Likewise, children who are born with normal health conditions but who lack much verbal, visual, physical, or emotional stimulation have to be given extra time and care to nurture them and to pull them up from this early brain void.

Your environment teaches throughout your life. It is impossible to learn in a void. Everything around you teaches. Each of your senses is gathering information constantly, without your having to think about it. So, it makes sense that by providing an enriched environment for learning, you are stimulating thought processes and creating an optimum learning opportunity.

For several decades Marian Diamond and others have been conducting research at the University of California at Berkeley on enriching the environment for learning. Most of her now-famous studies were done with rats, but research now determines the findings from her studies extend to the human brain as well.

This information has had a major impact on brain research and teaching/learning. When you invite students into an environment that is rich with stimulants for the brain, learning happens. When you invite students into a sterile, dull, or rigid environment, learning is hampered. This statement applies to students of all ages. Brains deprived of interesting stimulation suffer from atrophy. Dendrites shrivel, and the brain begins to slow down. Interestingly enough when the brain is provided with stimulation, both physical and intellectual, it continues to grow and flourish well into old age.

Several years ago I was leading a session of a national training event in New Jersey. The training was in late March (important detail). The classroom that was assigned to me was a youth room. My first thought was to make immediate changes in the learning environment. Fortunately, my second thought was to let the room teach. When my students entered the room and were settled, I asked them to look around and tell me what the room said to them. They looked at me strangely for a minute and then it hit them. One participant said, "This room says I don't care about you." We made a list of all the things that created this message in the room. Some of the items were an old dusty Christmas tree propped in one corner (remember this is late March), Christmas cards dangling from one corner in the windows, candy wrappers on the floor, window blinds hanging at odd angles—you get the picture. The room did indeed say loud and clear, "I don't care about you." Think about what your room says.

I like to have students create the room. It helps them take ownership and claim their space. Many churches share space, so that is a consideration that may not allow you to get too elaborate. And elaborate is not always better. Some churches go overboard and create environments with too much stimulation. Finding a happy medium that works for you and your students is what it is all about.

Pleasant surroundings with adequate light, temperature, furniture, and acoustics is an invaluable learning setting. When any of these conditions are at odds with the students' needs, learning is impaired. If students are too cold/hot or lighting is insufficient or seating is not size appropriate, they will focus on meeting their body's physical needs. Learning gets placed on a back burner.

Abraham Maslow's "Hierarchy of Needs" tells us that our physical and psychological needs must be met first before any higher level of intellect can become engaged. Set up your room to meet as many comfort needs as possible to help the brain focus on learning content.

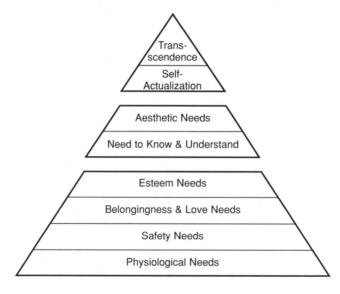

Figure 9

You can create your room to serve as an advanced organizer by setting up props, pictures, or music for your lesson. When students enter your room and their senses are engaged, the brain kicks into sorting the stimuli and making connections immediately. You do not learn in a void. Everything in your room stimulates thinking; set it up to your advantage.

The environment needs to meet the students' academic needs as well as their comfort and sensory needs. If your students enjoy researching topics, find as many resource books as you can. Some basics to include might be a Bible dictionary, concordance, maps of biblical lands, life and times books, a book of biblical characters, and a list of biblical Web sites. These references should keep your most Logical/Mathematical students and your Sensing types happy. Encourage them to complete further research; it will help them and those who hear the information to learn at a deeper level.

We have already touched on emotional environment, but it bears repeating. Make certain, to the very best of your ability, that there is an atmosphere of safety and a minimum of threat. This is probably the most important thing you can do to promote learning. Consider the research being done on school violence. It points irrefutably to the bullying, putdowns, and lack of self-esteem suffered by the perpetrators of school violence. Such an environment is an attack on personhood and must not be tolerated at any age.

Action Research

What does your room say?

How do you incorporate sensory enrichment in your environment to engage the brain?

How have you met the physical comfort needs of your students?

How have you met the intellectual needs of your students?

Check page 33 to see if any information here appeared in your best/worst learning list.

Application 6

Self-directed learning leads
to increased involvement.

Try this exercise: Close your eyes and recall a time when you had a voice in your own learning. Were you more or less engaged in learning when you had a part in planning it? How did it feel?

Then think of a time where everything was pre-programmed for you, where the presenter alone decided what you needed to know. How did it feel? Did you have any time to get your learning needs met? How? When? Were your questions answered to your specific needs?

Brain research confirms that students who have a say in what they are learning are more tuned in to the learning process. This concept of active involvement in learning and self-directed learning is referred to as "scaffolding." Think of a metaphor: A scaffold is erected at the beginning of a building project. It provides the framework and structure for the building. As the building takes on its shape, the scaffold is removed and the building stands alone. You are the scaffold. You are there to provide framework and structure. As your students grow in trust and confidence, you can take a lesser role as facilitator and let them direct and participate in their own learning. I'm sure some of you are saying, "Right! They expect me to have the lessons done and ready to teach them." Some folks do seem to want you to be in charge of their learning. This is called passive learning, where they sit and listen and you provide the information. This is an old model of teaching/learning. We know now this method is not very effective in creating deep thinking and true learning.

I like to begin an ongoing Bible study class with the statement, "I am not the keeper of the answers." I see my job more as facilitator of process and encourage shared learning. Brain research says learning is more effective if students are involved in solving their own problems and answering their own questions. When students are part of the discovery, learning becomes more deeply imprinted.

It would be ever so much easier if, each time there was a question in Bible study, the teacher provided the answer. This process is potentially harmful, however, in at least three ways: (1) It assumes there is one right answer; (2) it assumes students do not have the ability to make their own discoveries; and (3) it shuts down any further discussion or differing opinions. This effectively shuts students down in their thinking process. They have no input and no personal investment in the answer.

In the first session of a seminary course on Christian education, students were invited to list their learning needs in this field. One student became upset and commented that he was paying too much for this course not to be told what he needed. We explained that there was indeed a structured syllabus with pertinent information. There were also some time slots that were specifically unstructured to be filled in according to the needs of the students. This was a totally new concept to him (and the rest of the class). Once he heard the responses of other students, he became aware of the importance of the strategy and in the end was grateful.

Involving students in this way may initially be uncomfortable. Ease your students into developing their own learning through small changes. It may not happen overnight, but slowly they will begin to see that their learning is enhanced and enriched when they take some ownership of it. Remember Application 2, the brain is designed to create meaning. If your students have some learning needs that are not met, they may become frustrated and tune out.

Your primary job as facilitator is to help students learn and grow in their own faith. Including students in their own learning may be a new approach for you and for your students. It may not be easy at first. If you have been comfortable with providing answers and your students look to you for answers, you will create a level of discomfort. This discomfort is sometimes referred to as growing pains. If it causes too much discomfort, someone may drop out. Often really good teaching/learning involves risk taking. Check in with your students on a regular basis to learn their comfort levels.

To integrate this brain research into your classroom, you can invite students of all ages into your decision-making process. Children can be invited to make choices about which they might like to do first, see the video or read the story. Setting boundaries and allowing for choices help develop priorities, practice coming to consensus, and encourage problem solving and critical thinking practices—all part of the learning process.

For adults, being invited to participate in their learning gives them some ownership and allows them to design a program direction that meets their needs. I'm not suggesting you throw out the curriculum. I am suggesting that you offer choices, make group assignments where students can select a project they want to participate in, offer independent study options for those who want to dig deeper into research, and allow students to select from a variety of activities. Adults are there because they want to be. Make the experience the best it can be for them.

I taught an adult Bible study class from a standard thirteen-week curriculum piece that lasted for over seven months. We used the curriculum, just took side trips and delved deeper into some of the aspects. My students often became so immersed in the story and wanting/needing to make further inquiries and connections that the lessons took on a life of their own. The students directed their own learning, which became much more in-depth than the curriculum could do alone. It was fascinating to observe the faith growth as they explored concepts and made discoveries.

These students did not want nor expect me to be the keeper of the answers or to feed them information. They were sophisticated adults who were on a spiritual journey. This course was a major stepping stone on that journey. They tested ideas, refuted some concepts, and made their own discoveries. They wanted to know. Because of the duration of this study and the careful structuring of ground rules, they grew to trust one another. This trust led to faith sharing that was a delight to behold.

Action Research

How do you involve students in making decisions about their learning?

Reflect on your teaching/learning style. Would you consider your teaching leadership style to be more like
a gardener tending plants?
a captain of a ship?
a map maker?
a compass pointing to true north?
a guide?
a pathfinder?
a cruise director?

Check page 33 to see if this concept fits into your best/worst scenario.

Application 7

Provide intellectual challenge that is not too difficult or too easy.

Try this exercise: Close your eyes and recall a time when an assignment was given that was far beyond your ability. You did not have enough information or reference materials to support your learning. How did it feel? Or perhaps the reverse is true. You were asked to report on something so trivial or basic that you felt no need to complete any further work. How did that feel?

In order to keep your brain learning and functioning at optimum performance, you need to provide new experiences that keep the brain challenged. This kind of activity stimulates dendrite growth and keeps the brain functioning well. We know that the brain learns differently when new concepts are introduced. More electrical and chemical energy is required to make new connections than to revisit preexisting connections.

If students feel the challenge is beyond them, they will give up and tune out. If they feel there is not enough challenge, they tune out because there is nothing to excite them and keep them interested. Your job as teacher/facilitator is to offer a variety of activities at different levels. For instance, you know music is an important factor in learning. To some students, being asked to write a song about the lesson would be totally beyond their perceived ability. They would opt out. For others, to create a new song would be a neat and fun challenge. For still others, it would be no challenge; they would become bored. So, you offer choices. You can have several musical activities, including researching music already written about the lesson topic, writing new words to a familiar song or hymn tune about the lesson, or composing a new song to teach the lesson. The point is, you offer choices. Students will select the activity that challenges them at a comfortable level. Everyone wins. You have a variety of musical enrichments, your students have some input into their level of learning, and you have offered challenges at various comfort levels.

You can offer another level of challenge by varying your methods of teaching. Keep your lesson fresh by switching gears every so often. Change from large-group to small-group work. Take field trips (they can be to the fellowship hall). Invite guest speakers.

Offer challenges by including problem-solving activities, critical-thinking exercises, complex activities, and projects that relate to your study.

Choices and variety of activities will keep your students challenged in ways that will keep their dendrites sparking. Varieties of resources will help make these challenges positive. If students have questions and nowhere to find answers, they may become frustrated. Make sure you have basic resources such as a Bible dictionary, a concordance, a Bible commentary, and some books with graphics including maps and historical information. Have available one of the videos out there that depict biblical lands and historical teachings.

Having a Bible "expert" in your class may be a plus or a minus. Sometimes this person is a wonderful fount of knowledge and offers just enough of an answer to point the other students in a discovery direction. If, however, this person wants everyone to know about his or her "expertness," he or she will be more than happy to provide the rest of the class with the "right" answer. This is not a blessing. Then students have no challenge to make their own discoveries. If the "right" answer is always provided, students have no part in the struggle to learn. They do not have to tax or challenge their brains at all.

Action Research

How do you challenge your students?

How can you determine if a challenge is too difficult or too easy?

How can you meet the different needs for challenge in your classroom?

Check page 33 to see if any of these aspects are reflected in your best/worst scenarios.

Application 8

The brain collects data through all your senses.

Try this exercise: Enter a room that you are familiar with and that has no obstructions that could cause danger. Close your eyes, and negotiate getting across the room. What happened? Were you able to do it? How? What other senses did you use?

Most people rely heavily on two senses: sight and sound. We get most of our data through what we see and hear. I would like to suggest that you add another dimension to your teaching/learning experience by incorporating all your senses in the learning process. We know the first step in learning (a.k.a. long-term memory) is the collection of data through your sensory or immediate memory. I believe it will be beneficial to take a closer look at how your senses are involved with learning. You may be surprised.

Visual Sense. You receive information through all your senses. You receive over half of your information through this one sense alone. Eighty-six percent of adults say they are visual learners. Pictures, graphics, maps, slides, videos all help you imprint information in your brain.

Once this visual stimuli has been perceived in one of the various areas of your brain, it is connected to what you already know. This connection to previously recorded information is when meaning happens. You know through previous experience that blue is blue or a tree is a tree or a moving vehicle is coming toward you too fast. Most visual stimuli is processed through your occipital lobes, also known as visual cortex, located at the lower central back of your brain. (See Figure 4, page 30.) Through extensive study, researchers have discovered your visual sense is subdivided into different areas for processing the stimuli from your world. There are as many as thirty-five different visual areas that process movement, color, depth, distance, objects, and so forth. Studies done with monkeys have provided much of the most recent information.

Your brain is uniquely designed to sort stimuli and to discern what is important to you. Your brain can identify a friend in a crowded room or see the word *Jesus* in a set of black and white shapes. (See Figure 8, page 58.) This research explains why it is important to tell students ahead of time what to look for in a video or the kind of information you are looking for as the key to the story. Your brain anticipates and becomes focused on looking for specific information.

Have you ever said, "I can see it in my mind"? Visuals are powerful memory tools. They also help increase understanding. That is why I asked for graphics in this book. A picture is indeed worth at least a thousand words. The graphics I have suggested are for specific reasons. Each time I asked for one, it was to bring a point home in greater depth than words alone. I believe graphics would increase the interest and level of understanding in most any book. For one thing, graphics help you see a concept; they break up the page to create interest and novelty for your brain; and they help your brain focus.

Children's books often are ninety to one hundred percent pictures. Wordless books have become popular in children's literature. Children tell the story in their own creative way simply by looking at the pictures. Children begin to identify pictures with words. This concept works with symbols too. The most widely recognized symbol for two-year-olds is the golden arches. This symbol quickly becomes imprinted on their brains, and they make the connection to food. This concept is why businesses spend fortunes on company logos and why icons have become multimillion-dollar visual tools.

Books for older children and youth contain fewer pictures. Most adult books contain no pictures and few graphics. This is not the most efficient way of presenting material. Use visuals to increase and enhance understanding. Visuals are a critical tool for teaching at any age.

When visuals are unavailable, ask your students to see something in their "mind's eye." Helping them "see" something will add a greater depth of understanding to just about any lesson. Students pull out visual memories of related times and places and make connections to the new material.

Bring in objects for students to see. Find slides or videos to focus the brain, and allow stimuli to imprint on your brain from a multitude of entry points.

Encourage your students to draw or doodle. In creativity training I encourage students to draw a line down the middle of their paper. On the left side of the paper I ask them to take whatever notes they might deem important. On the right side of the paper I encourage them to draw pictures of what they hear. I have found this technique helps in imprinting the concepts of any lesson. Students do not always draw pictures of what is actually happening. Often they draw a picture that makes a brain connection for them. In one case the lesson was about Jesus feeding the five thousand. One of my students drew the golden arches and made the connection of feeding five thousand people today, every day. He went from there to how he could help feed the hungry. From a sketch, his brain made several leaps. It is a powerful learning tool. Many schools are using a similar tool called an "Interactive Notebook." One side of the notebook is for verbal notes, the opposite page may be a Venn Drawing or a Mind Map or other graphic organizer to replicate the same information in a visual way. The brain has twice the sensory input. Graphic organizers are important tools in helping students see the story or concept.

Transforming words into visual symbols is a fun and neat learning tool. The word *tall* can be written two inches tall on your paper, or *fast* can be written slanted forward with speed trails behind it. You get the picture. Your brain picks up the concept immediately. Just about any descriptive word and some creative thought produce a variety of word pictures.

Colors and shapes, large and small, light and darkness are all measured by your brain in the context of visual sense. You can create a mood with light. Anyone familiar with a Tenebrae Service understands the power of darkness. There is a sense of stillness and awe when all the candles have been extinguished. For many, the darkness captures the essence of the story as much as, if not more than, the actual words.

Use visual stimuli to increase understanding.

Auditory Sense. Most auditory information is processed through the temporal lobes, located just above your ears.

As you have come to expect, the processing is done in several subdivisions that carry out the various functions of hearing, including volume, pitch and timbre, and tone. This complex functioning is what allows you to distinguish one person's voice from another's. When you make a phone call, as often as not, you can tell who you are talking with through voice recognition. Voices are so unique, many security systems are now voice-activated. Ask any new mother about distinguishing her baby's cry from any other if you need further proof of this complex system.

This system functions differently in different people (the uniqueness factor again). Some students' ears are tuned to recognize perfect pitch; others can differentiate feelings in the tone or pitch of a person's voice ("I heard a cry in her voice," or "Don't talk to me in that tone of voice"). Your brain is attuned to incredible numbers of nuances in sound.

There are sounds all around you constantly. Try this exercise; close your eyes, remain absolutely silent and listen for thirty-four seconds. Record all the sounds you hear. It is amazing the sounds that are present all the time and that your brain tunes out. A clock ticking, birds, street noises, a door closing. Your brain has the power to focus on the sounds it needs to hear and to ignore all other extraneous sounds. If it did not do this, you could not function.

If you want to get your students' attention, abruptly change the tone or volume of your voice. Try whispering and see what happens in your classroom.

Use sound effects to heighten awareness. A friend said the most memorable Good Friday service he ever led included the sound of a hammer striking nails immediately following the Scripture reading about Jesus' crucifixion. Sound effects add a deeper level of understanding. As with the hammer, adding sound effects can bring a story home by connecting yet another set of entry points to your brain. The message becomes imprinted in the words as well as the other sounds that flesh out the story. Your brain is receiving enriched stimuli, which helps understanding.

We have already touched on the power of music to trigger emotion. Use music as a teaching tool. Use it to get the brain's attention, to establish a mood, to set a stage for learning. Music has the power to move students in time. Music can take you back to high school, to your wedding, to a funeral, to your new baby. It is a powerful auditory tool. Make sure to incorporate it into your teaching.

I love to watch the percussion section of an orchestra. The precision of playing a single set of notes can make or break a musical piece. A triangle or drums or bells at precisely the right moment gives new life to a musical rendition. It gets the brain's attention. Exactly the same procedure will get the attention of your students' brains. To signal "time's up" or to change the pace of the lesson, use a whistle, a horn, a triangle, or some auditory clue.

A caution: Use music for background during nonthinking tasks. Do not use music while students are involved in learning. When they need to do mental work, turn off the music. For many people it is a distraction, especially if it contains words. If you are trying to learn and to listen to music, your brain is involved in two separate learning modes at once. Students, particularly teens, do this all the time. They claim they cannot learn without their stereo playing. What is actually happening is the brain is tuning in and out of two separate learnings. In your classroom, use music as a before class mood enhancer or during breaks but not when students are learning.

These are the senses most widely used in your teaching/learning. Take time to read the following and consider incorporating your other senses into lessons as well.

Tactile Sense. The sense of touch is processed mainly in the parietal lobes, which are at the top of the brain. Each is comprised of different areas that control different parts of your tactile sense, such as your telling your muscles where and when to move or imprinting texture or temperature or where your body is in relation to your environment. Try this: Do not think of where your left foot is. Where does your brain automatically take you? To your left foot.

Tactile sensations can add a new depth to understanding when they are incorporated into your lesson. Tactile sense covers a broad spectrum of consideration.

Most people have experienced the "elevator syndrome." You get into an elevator with one other person and each of you moves to the farthest corners. You claim your own space. When someone gets too close (invades your space), you instinctively move back. Your brain needs to feel safe in its surroundings, including its own space. This is true of classroom space as well. If students feel too cramped, too close, their comfort level is tested and their brain may not be fully attentive.

If your room is too hot or too cold, your brain will instruct your body to make adjustments. You create a fan out of a bulletin or fold your arms to capture warmth. If seats are too hard or too low the brain is working to get comfortable and not to focus on the lesson. These are tactile considerations that have impact before the lesson even begins.

Once you begin the lesson, your sense of touch is important in giving the brain information. What does it feel like? Is it hot or cold, heavy or light, soft or hard? Providing objects to touch adds to the brain's understanding of what is being presented. Objects in the form of something to touch or hold as you tell the story help the brain understand. There are connections from the tips of your fingers to your brain. Touching a grain of wheat, sand, water, or any item connected to your lesson will give the brain additional input to aid understanding. Experiment with providing tactile items to enhance your lessons.

Toys or ordinary objects often help the brain to concentrate. Providing toys like Koosh® balls, Slinkys®, wands, or items like paperclips, pipe cleaners, or telephone wire (my favorite) is a neat way to keep your tactile sense engaged while the lesson is going on. It keeps hands busy, so the brain can function

Sense of Smell. The odors you smell, your olfactory sense, are sent to your cognitive centers in the cortex and then on to the limbic system. Brain research has discovered we are able to identify over ten thousand different odors. The scents/odors in your classroom can evoke emotional memories and/or draw people in. Pleasant fragrances cause people to be calmer, become more efficient, and/or increase mental agility. Research at the Smell and Taste Treatment and Research Foundation in Chicago suggests brain wave frequencies can be changed by smell. Much new research is being done on the sense of smell. Experiments with more efficient working conditions, earlier recovery from illness, sales and marketing, and relaxation are all being centered around scents. Consider the smell of freshly brewed coffee or freshly baked bread or apple pie with cinnamon. These will pull people into your room.

Humans have known for thousands of years that smell affects the brain. Aromatherapy is not a new concept. Various cultures have used aromatic herbs and spices for eons. Frankinscense and myrrh, of wise men fame, are aromatic pitches used for burial anointing. You can often purchase these items (you are on your own for gold!) at a Christian bookstore. Pass them around as you retell the story of Epiphany for a deeper level of learning. Once more, you are adding neural connections to your brain's memory bank.

Think of a smell that immediately brings a person or place to mind. My grandmother put dried lavender in the bedding to enhance sleep. This was long before aromatherapy. I never smell lavender without thinking of her. Your mother, aunt, or grandmother may have had a particular scent about her. Your father or uncle or grandfather may have smoked a pipe, and you recall him whenever you smell pipe smoke. Smells bring us back by opening neural pathways to memory.

Placing scented candles in your room may promote relaxation, but be certain to check with your students about allergies before incorporating any aromas.

We know that most foods taste the way we smell them. Sound strange? I have a friend who had sinus problems and could not smell for a month. He discovered he could not taste anything either. Your sense of taste is totally wrapped up in your sense of smell. Try holding your nose the next time you eat something that smells wonderful. These two senses are connected by your brain.

Sense of Taste. Your sense of taste is closely associated with emotional memory: Consider "comfort food." When you share a meal, your visual, olfactory, and tactile senses are all involved. Often there is an emotional quality that comes into play as well. Several of your senses are working together to contribute to your memory/learning.

Often religious traditions include meals—if not complete meals like Thanksgiving or a Seder, then symbolic meals like Holy Communion. Many biblical stories include food. Consider Abraham and Sarah. Sarah was preparing a meal for the strangers who predicted a child for her. Manna from heaven fed Moses' followers in the wilderness. Jesus ate a Passover meal with his disciples.

Connecting your sense of taste to a lesson adds additional sensory input. Find a good biblical cookbook and experiment with different foods. Share their place in the Bible as you experience particular stories.

Connecting the pleasurable act of sharing a meal (snack) in your classroom brings students together. Chatting over a cup of coffee is an important part of learning fellowship. Taking meals to bereaved members or new mothers or someone recovering from an illness says we care.

Encourage meals or snacks both as an interesting addition to your lesson and as a time of sharing your lives informally. We had a Sunday school class that was called "Grounds for Discussion." This group met each Sunday around the coffee pot and shared their lives and faith.

Some studies suggest that if you eat a specific food when you are studying and eat the same food when recalling the information, it will be easier to recall. My friends think this is a great excuse to eat chocolate during Bible study. Works for me too.

Your students will benefit when you incorporate as many sensory stimuli as you can in your lessons. The more senses you incorporate, the more efficient learning becomes. Each stimuli is recorded in different areas of the brain. The more pathways you establish, the more your memory can pull on to recreate that learning. Incorporating multisensory activities throughout life hedges bets against the inevitable loss of some memory as you age. If you have five places to pull a memory from, there is less chance of losing it totally.

The bottom line: Incorporate as many senses as possible in your lessons to enhance learning.

Action Research

Consider your last few lessons. Which senses did you incorporate?

How do you/might you incorporate senses into your lessons?

List three ways you can include the sense of touch in your lessons.

Have you checked for allergies/asthma among your students?

Try the experiments suggested to heighten your own awareness of your sensual environment.

Ask your students about their comfort level in the room.

Check page 33 to see if any of these sensory conditions appear on your best/worst list.

Application 9

The brain can process limited amounts of information at a time.

Try this exercise: Close your eyes and recall a time when you were presented with so much information your brain shut down. This phenomenon is a common occurrence in today's world and is referred to as information overload. How did you feel?

We know that more is not always better. Presenting too much information or presenting it too quickly shuts down optimal brain function.

Seven is one of the holy numbers of the Bible. There is probably good reason for this. For the brain, seven appears to be a holy number as well. Research by George A. Miller and others declares the brain can only learn so much information at one time. The number of items, whether it be words, numbers, or letters, the brain can learn at one time is seven (plus or minus two).

Please try another experiment: Read the names of the books of the Torah and focus on them. Spend about ten seconds trying to memorize them:

Genesis
Exodus
Leviticus
Numbers
Deuteronomy

After ten seconds close your eyes and try to recall the books in order. How did you do? If you are like the average person, you could repeat the books in order without much difficulty. If you already know all the books of the Bible in order, this exercise does not count. List any other five books of the Bible. Focus on them. Commit them to memory. Then close your eyes and repeat them in order.

Now, try the same experiment with the names of the twelve disciples:

Peter
Andrew
James
John

Philip
Bartholomew
Thomas
Matthew
James
Thaddaeus
Simon
Judas

Focus on the names. Commit them to memory. After ten seconds, close your eyes and try to recall the twelve names. How did you do? Unless you already knew the names, you might have had a more difficult time with this exercise. Why? Because the list was more than the holy number of seven.

Try another experiment. Read the Ten Commandments below:

You shall have no other gods before me.
You shall not worship graven images.
You shall not take the name of God in vain.
You shall keep the sabbath holy.
You shall honor your mother and father.
You shall not kill.
You shall not commit adultery.
You shall not steal.
You shall not bear false witness against your neighbor.
You shall not covet your neighbor's property.

Focus on them. Take forty-five seconds to commit them to memory. Close your eyes and repeat as many as you can in the correct order. How did you do? Unless you already knew them, it was not an easy task.

Try it again, this time focus on the first four *honoring God*:

You shall have no other gods before me.
You shall not worship graven images.
You shall not take the name of God in vain.
You shall keep the sabbath holy.

Now focus on the next six *honoring others*:

You shall honor your mother and father.
You shall not kill.
You shall not commit adultery

You shall not steal.

You shall not bear false witness against your neighbor.

You shall not covet your neighbor's property.

Focus. Take forty-five seconds to commit them to memory. Close your eyes and repeat them again. How did you do this time? More than likely you did better.

So, what do these exercises have to do with teaching/learning? Plenty. Your brain has a limited working memory. By becoming aware of this phenomenon, you can plan your lessons accordingly. It serves no purpose and may be detrimental to attempt to include too much information at one time.

In the first exercise, you were asked to commit five books of the Bible to memory. It was a relatively easy task because it falls into the holy number "seven" rule. Your brain was able to incorporate those names with little difficulty. The next exercise, remembering the names of Jesus' twelve disciples exceeded the seven rule; and it became a more difficult task. In the Ten Commandments exercise, when you were told to look at the commandments as a whole unit, it was more difficult than when you broke them into two categories. This is called "chunking."

When you plan your lessons, read them over carefully and be aware of the holy seven rule. Do not attempt to load more information than the brain can handle learning at one time. Consider quality vs. quantity.

Take time with a lesson. Break it into manageable chunks. If there is interest in a particular Scripture verse, take it apart and put it back together again. Check it out in several versions to compare choices of words. Look up specific words. Don't try to rush through Scripture study. The brain can only process so much information at a time. Relax. Reflect. Review, and learn it in depth.

Action Research

Try these exercises with your students. Invite them to reflect on the experience and elicit discoveries from them.

Think of other areas where the holy seven rule applies (telephone numbers, social security numbers, others).

Find the number seven in the Bible. Consider why and where the number occurs. Make some conclusions as to why you think the number was used.

Check page 33 and see if this concept was present in your best or worst learning scenario.

Application 10

To get the brain's attention, change pace.

Try this exercise: Close your eyes and recall a time when you have been aware of something in your environment that captures your attention. It may be traffic noise or a bell signaling the opening of an elevator door or anything that causes you to stop and think (perhaps in annoyance).

As you think about this attention-grabbing thing, consider what happens when you are in this environment for a long period of time. If you are like most folks, your brain tunes it out after a period of time. It no longer holds any import or interest.

I live about twenty miles from the Rochester airport. Our home is directly under the southern approach to runway 8. When we first moved here, every plane that flew overhead got my attention. I was aware of each incoming plane. Now more than three years later, I seldom notice the planes. Guests will comment, and I am surprised that they take notice. My brain has totally tuned out the interruptions to my thought process.

This information translates to your teaching in the fact that if you want to get the attention of your students' brains, introduce something novel. Change the pace of what you are doing. This is a fairly simple matter once you become aware of it. Changing pace can be anything that breaks the routine of what you are currently doing. Some of the options may be as simple as:

* calling for a "turn and talk with a partner for two minutes and thirteen seconds"—I always tack on an odd number of seconds; it stirs interest and makes students chuckle. They usually wait with amusement to see what odd time frame I will give them next;

* using a video clip;

* turning out the lights;

* playing music;

* using a continuum across the room and having students stand where their answer is;

* small group work;
* inviting students to think about a similar experience;
* using a "sword drill" technique (For some of you this is a new concept; sword drills are timed experiences of locating a Scripture passage. Everyone begins with a closed Bible. A Scripture verse is presented, say Proverbs 15:3. The first person [or person on a team] to find it and read it gets points.);
* using a concordance to locate a key word in a Scripture passage for comparison;
* asking for sixty-seven seconds of silence;
* talking in a whisper;
* introducing a guest in costume;
* taking a "bio break" (A bio break is anything your biological system needs—to eat, to drink, to move, to stand, or to use a restroom facility);
* taking a brain break (see Section Four for a list of various brain breaks, page 130).

These are but a few examples of changing the pace of what you are doing. This application is vital for holding the brain's attention. Go to page 33 and check your list of "worst" learning experiences. In my experience of leading groups in a study of brain research, "lecturing too long" almost always makes the list.

There was a judge in Buffalo who would take breaks during a long trial. His comment was always, "Ladies and gentlemen, we are going to take a five-minute recess because the brain cannot comprehend what the fanny cannot endure." He was ever so right. Long periods of sitting or any activity that is ongoing causes the brain to shift into a lower learning pace. Physical evidence of this phenomenon is eyes not focused, slouching posture, doodling, staring into space, yawning. You know what it looks like. Evidence of any of these behaviors should be your cue to change pace. Your students are no longer focused on what you are doing. You have lost them. You need to do something novel to recapture their attention.

Researchers have discovered that twenty minutes is maximum for one type of activity. This does not mean you have to change topics, it simply means to change activities by using one or more of the suggestions listed or by creating your own methods of changing pace.

Back to my opening statement in this application. Changing pace and novelty work when you want to get the brain's attention. However, just as I no longer am aware of the planes approaching runway 8, if you do the same thing too often, the brain tunes it out. Even novelty becomes less effective. Keep it fresh, but do not use novelty too often. Usually, teaching sessions on Sunday range from forty-five minutes to an hour. That will mean one or two at the most changes of pace are essential. In a longer session you will need more changes, of course. Do not use the same activities each session. Vary your activities, and you will hold your students' attention.

Action Research

Invite your students to share their feelings and thoughts about a long, continuous activity. Tell them about this finding and check their reaction.

Review the list of suggestions for change-of-pace activities. Record at least three of your own.

Review your lessons and look for optimum places to change pace.

Check page 33 to see if this application was addressed.

Application 11

Reflection time is critical
to understanding.

Try this exercise: Close your eyes and recall a time when you left a class and your brain was so full of information you could not remember most of it. You were experiencing information overload. How did it feel?

Hearing something and understanding it are two totally different things. Understanding does not occur until what you have heard is processed through your brain, neural connections are made, and new information is imprinted in long-term memory and can be retrieved at will. Understanding is an internal process.

If you want students to understand something, you need to give them time to process new information and to make the connections. If they are listening the entire time, there is no opportunity for the brain to process the information. You must allow "down time" and reflection time for the brain to process information. Revisit Section Two for how the processing takes place.

Time is the operative word. Often it seems the hour is so short and there is so much to cover, you try to cram it all in during one session because next week there is the next lesson. WRONG!

When you fill the hour with providing information and do not allow time for this information to be processed, understanding cannot happen. What you have provided is a lot of words with little or no meaning attached. Meaning or understanding is an internal process. It cannot happen when the brain is engaged in external activities such as listening and note taking. Your students can be either listening (external) or making meaning (internal). They cannot do both at the same time.

You must provide down time for the neural connections to be made and synapses strengthened. It is similar to the way your body processes food. If you just kept putting food in your mouth, without taking time to chew properly and swallow, your digestive system would not work correctly; and you would not get the nutritional benefit of the food.

Quiet time, reflection time, incubation time is critical to learning. This is not down time for your brain. Actually it is the busiest time for your brain as it makes all those important connections. When you provide new information, allow several minutes of reflection. This may be a new concept and some students (or teachers) may sense discomfort. Those who are used to pushing through the hour to get everything done will be most disconcerted. They may see it as a waste of their time. Action research again. Invite them into the process. Explain the fact that the brain needs time to make connections. As with any change in teaching/learning approach, take small steps.

Invite students to write notes about the information or to discuss with partners or in small groups what they have just heard. Allow them time to process and solidify the information. Each of these strategies helps the brain create or strengthen neural pathways. Writing or talking with someone about the new information strengthens the connections.

We know that about twenty minutes for adults, less for children, is the optimum time for information input. Take a quick break and/or change the pace of learning. Allow for reflection. If for some reason this incubation/reflection time is impossible during class time, encourage students to write or go over notes or talk with someone about the lesson as soon as possible after the session.

One of the best ways to insure that learning has taken place is to have your students teach this information to one another or to someone else. "You learn best by teaching" is a truism. If you can't explain it to someone else, you haven't learned it.

I like to close a teaching session by having the last minutes—the length of time is proportional to the entire class time—to reflect on what the students have learned. There are at least one hundred six ways to do this. I'll share some of mine; I'm sure you have your own ideas.

Some strategies for reflection for a Sunday school class:

* create symbols of the learning from telephone wire or pipe cleaners;

* think of a word that captures the essence of the lesson today;

* name one learning that could change your life if you practiced it;

* select a color that symbolizes your learning today; explain;

* state a connection you made from today's lesson to your experience.

Some strategies for reflection for an ongoing class or retreat:

* stand in front of the large piece of paper (saved and posted from each session) that was most meaningful for you; explain;

*create a word for each letter in the name of something you learned;

* write a poem or story about your learning;

* find or create a symbol that expresses your learning;

* provide a box of "stuff" and invite students to make metaphorical connections;

* write words to a familiar tune to express what you have learned.

You get the idea. The point is this step is CRITICAL for learning to happen. Often teachers wonder why students do not remember what has been taught. Not allowing time to reflect and connect is one of the right answers to that query. If you alter nothing else in your teaching/learning, make this change. You will see tremendous growth in understanding.

It is also helpful to begin your session by reviewing what you did last time. This needs to take only a few minutes. It will reconnect the brain and get it ready to add new information to pathways that are receptive. Recalling information strengthens synapses. Remember the more often you make connections, the easier it is to remember them.

Action Research

How often do you allow time to reflect?

What might you do if you meet resistance to reflection time?

List some strategies you might use to help students reflect.

Check page 33 to see if this information connects with your best/worst experience.

Application 12

Hands-on learning is minds-on learning.

Try this exercise: Close your eyes and recall a time when you were totally involved in learning. You were so into it, you lost track of time. How did it feel?

Educators have known forever that the best learning is when you do it. The earliest forms of teaching were through apprenticeships. To learn anything from a trade to how to prepare food, students signed on with an expert in the field or with their mother, father, or the local baker or blacksmith. Students observed the master, then began to take small parts in the process, then took on more and more of the responsibility until they became proficient. Much of that direct teaching has been lost to us due to time and numbers of students. In some areas it still exists. From personal experience, I can say I learned more in my student teaching experience than in all the course work I did throughout college. I worked with a master teacher and was given more and more responsibility as the term went on. I worked directly with the children. Rather than reading about theory in a book, I was actually doing it.

John Dewey and the Progressive Education movement suggested that the best learning was learning that could be used in life experience. Brain research supports this truism in several ways. When you are involved in doing, your whole body and therefore your whole brain is involved. You see, hear, touch, smell what you are doing. Information is being imprinted in one hundred ways to your brain. Memories are created and meaning is made by being involved in decision making, problem solving, finding or creating necessary materials, working with others, shared responsibility. All these factors are stored in your brain, and connections are made and remade as the experience unfolds.

How does this information affect your classroom? You engage your students in hands-on/minds-on learning as often as possible. Instead of sitting and listening, get them up and involved.

Create items that pertain to your lesson. Make a mural, create a tent to meet in, take a field trip, write a skit, create a song, bake unleavened bread. Do a service project, visit a nursing home, feed the hungry, work at a soup kitchen, collect toys for needy children (not just at Christmas), knit lap robes for nursing homes. The ideas are endless. The point is, get your students involved.

This kind of learning is much closer to what Jesus did than simply listening to someone speak about God's word. In the Book of James we read, "Be doers of the word, and not merely hearers" (1:22).

If this seems too much of a stretch for your class, then at least get them involved in the lesson in smaller ways. Invite them to do additional research, roleplay a story, create a contemporary version of a Bible story, create props to tell the story.

Passive learning is well named. Students simply sit and listen. Sometimes they learn something. Often it is not meaningful nor is it remembered for too long. I worked with a class of older adults who were used to sitting and listening to someone speak about the Bible. I got them (not all of them) involved in the story of Mary and Martha. I did a visualization where they became each of the sisters and experienced the story in their mind's eye. They then wrote a short letter as Mary or Martha telling someone of their experience. It was a powerful lesson. One of the ladies stopped me after class and said, "You know, I never knew you could learn so much from such a short piece of Scripture." Get students involved!

Action Research

How do you get students actively involved in your lessons?

What might you do in your sessions to increase hands-on/minds-on learning?

Think of three reasons you believe hands-on/minds-on learning is an effective teaching/learning strategy.

Check page 33 to see if this information appears in your best/worst experience.

Section Four

A Bonus

———

This section is a bonus. It is for those of you who want to know more. I have provided:

* **Brain Breaks** that I use to change pace and re-energize the brain. Play with mine; then create your own. It is vital to take brain breaks.

* **Elaborations** on some of the things I wrote about: FYI things.

* **Alphabetical Applications** for lifelong brain fitness: I use this as a handout. It is succinct and works well as an introduction to brain research.

* **Suggestions** for parents, grandparents, and other caregivers to increase brain power. You are not in this alone. There are many things beyond a Sunday school classroom to raise awareness of boosting brain power.

* **Resources** that I have used to compile this book. They provide much more in-depth information than could possibly be contained here. The world of brain research is expanding so rapidly that there will be additional resources constantly. When I first became interested in brain research about five years ago, there were five books on the psychology shelf relating to the brain. Recently, I counted forty-three. My guess is that the number will increase consistently with the growing fascination with this topic. I have included videos and Web sites as well.

Brain Breaks

In any learning situation, your brain needs to take breaks. Depending on the length of your session, you may need to take one or more brain breaks. If you recall the application on limiting the amount of information your brain can handle (Application 9, page 113), you will recall the concept of "chunking"—introducing no more than seven (plus or minus two) pieces of information at a time. Also recall the application about reflection (Application 11, page 121) and realize you must stop periodically to let the brain absorb the information to avoid overload.

Brain breaks can be anything from simple to complex. The following are some brain breaks I use in my training. Some are adapted from *The Brain Gym,* by Gail and Paul Dennison (see Resources, page 138); others I have made up and use depending on the situation. All serve the purpose of changing your pace; some are intentional to activate both hemispheres of the brain. Reflect on those you would feel comfortable incorporating into your sessions, then come up with your own. I shall attempt to make some order of them.

Oxygenating exercises: get the blood pumping and oxygen flowing to the brain.

    * Stand and stretch for forty-seven seconds.

    * Stand on a continuum to physically take a stand on an issue, from one strong opinion to an opposite strong opinion. (Stretch the continuum across your classroom.)

    * Stand. Move to a place where you can stretch your arms out and not touch anyone else. With palms upward, make little movements to lift your arms upward thirty times. Then turn palms down, and make little movements to push your arms downward thirty times. Then turn palms to the front. Repeat, moving forward thirty times. Last, turn palms to the back; and move backward thirty times.

    * Stand and move to music.

    * Stand and march in place or around the room.

Bilateral exercises: get both hemispheres of the brain integrated.

    * Stand and walk around the room in a clockwise movement for

fifty-six seconds; then reverse your walk to counterclockwise for another fifty-six seconds.

* Stand and walk in a figure eight for seventy-two seconds while considering a question.

* Stand up and, with your right hand, make three sideways figure eights, beginning top right in front of you. Then make three sideways figure eights, beginning top left in front of you. Now repeat the exercise with your left hand.

* Stand up and write (not print) your name in the air in front of you as large as you can.

* Stand up and, with both hands, doodle in the air or on a large piece of paper.

* Stand up and, with both hands extended in front of you and beginning at the top, make large C's with both hands simultaneously (one will be backward).

These movements are designed to activate both hemispheres of the brain and/or cross the midline, which calls the brain to attention.

Novelty exercises: kicks the brain into paying attention.

* Write your name or a phrase from your Scripture passage with the opposite hand from the one you normally use.

* Stand and tap the top of your head with one hand and rub your stomach with the other hand simultaneously for thirty-three seconds. Repeat with the opposite hands.

* Turn a paper upside down and read it.

* Switch seats after a break.

* Teach from the back of the room.

* Switch your classroom routine.

Puzzle exercises: get the brain thinking in a different mode.

* Find puzzles in books or newspapers.

* Find hidden words puzzles (or make up your own).

* Create word jumbles (use words from your lesson).

Breathing exercises: control of breath calms the brain and gives it an oxygen boost.

* Practice taking three deep breaths and holding them for eleven seconds each.

* Practice "Yoga breathing" where you take a deep breath, hold it, and exhale slowly and only through your nose.

* Take a breath prayer break. (A breath prayer is a simple prayer that begins with a name for God and ends with a request: you say God's name as you breathe in and your request as you breathe out.) My favorite breath prayer is "Gracious God" (breathe in), "grant me your peace" (breathe out). Repeat your prayer three times slowly.

Relaxation exercises: calm the brain and quiet the soul.

* Press your palms and fingers together as hard as you can in front of your chest. Take three deep breaths. Return to neutral (lay hands flat in your lap). Then repeat for a total of three times.

* Cross your left ankle over your right. Cross your left wrist over your right. Twist your hands around and interlace your fingers. Bring your folded hands together toward your chest as far as you can. Hold this position and breathe slowly.

* Tighten all the muscles in your toes; hold for six seconds. Tighten all the muscles in your calves; hold for six seconds. Work your way all the way up your body (thighs, buttocks, stomach, scrunch your shoulders, tighten hands and arms, scrunch your face up to your eyes). If you have time, repeat the exercise moving from your eyes down to your toes. This is a fantastic exercise to totally relax the body and calm the brain.

Elaborations and Practical Suggestions

Remembering Names

A fun way of associating names if you are in a group setting where not everyone knows everyone else is a name game. There are many around. My favorite is one in which the leader begins and every person in a circle must state their name and an adjective that begins with the same first letter. I am "busy Barbara." The next person repeats my information then adds his or her adjective and name. The group hears each person's name several times as well as making a connection with an adjective. The leader ends the game by going completely around the circle, correctly naming everyone. Be careful what adjectives you choose, however. Nearly ten years after I led a group in this name game, there is a delightful woman in my church who is still known as "naughty Norma." The brain remembers!

Unless you use an exercise similar to the one just stated, remembering names of a group of people will be difficult. Working memory can only retain a certain amount of information at one time. (See Application 9, page 113.)

Making Connections

Try this memory experience for yourself and then with your students. On a plain piece of paper write the word "GOD" in the center of the paper. Set a timer for two minutes and thirty-four seconds. Write as many words that are connected to God as you think of in that time period. When the time is up, go back over your paper and draw lines connecting thoughts. Debrief by sharing with a partner or in small groups. I have used it with various groups from confirmation to adult retreats. It is a powerful, visual, and nonthreatening way to extract memories as the brain makes connections. This exercise works well as an advanced organizer. Select a key word and use it at the beginning of a new topic or lesson. (See Application 2, page 55.)

An Alphabet of Actions for Life-Long Brain Fitness

A - Alternate ways of doing everyday activities to keep your brain's attention.

B - Balance your life with work and play.

C - Challenge yourself with new and unique experiences.

D - Develop your senses—pay attention to sights, smells, sounds, tastes, touches every day.

E - Enjoy life to the fullest each day.

F - Find a cause to work for—passion is good for the brain.

G - Grow a garden—become a co-creator with God.

H - Home in on humor—laugh each day—especially at yourself.

I - Invest time in learning something new—create new neural connections.

J - Join a group—find new folks with whom to share your life.

K - Keep working at what you enjoy—life without joy is not brain friendly.

L - Love someone or something—the good chemicals you produce do wonders for your brain.

M - Memories mean a lot—treasure yours, they comprise who YOU are.

N - Notice something new every day—keep those dendrites firing.

O - Open your mind and heart to lots of right answers—don't shut down your thinking.

P - Play.

Q - Question things—ask what if? and why?

R - Reduce stress—stress over time is harmful to your brain.

S - Sing, in the shower and elsewhere.

T - Type onto the Internet—it keeps mind and hands busy.

U - Use all things in moderation.

V - Vary your activities—take brain breaks.

W - Water is necessary for brain health—drink eight glasses each day.

X - (e)Xercise.

Y - Yesterdays—recall them and share your memories.

Z - Zzz's—catch some with a cat nap.

Some Thoughts on Increasing Brain Power for Parents, Grandparents, and Other Care Providers

We know providing an environment that is rich and inviting can mold, shape, and literally create a child's brain. By providing some or many of the following possibilities you are doing more for this child's future than all the things money can buy. Many of the following suggestions are value based and cost little or no money. Remember you have the awesome responsibility and privilege of helping create children's brains and providing a lifetime of memories for them to draw upon.

Creating foundational spiritual memories becomes, to a great extent, a shared responsibility. One hour per week in Sunday school will not keep the religious memory alive. Parents must create reinforcement by asking their children to retell and reflect on the biblical stories. Questions such as, What did you learn in Sunday school today? often produce less-than-satisfying answers. To get a more complete and brain building answer, parents might start with comments and questions such as, Tell me the most important things you did in Sunday school to show God's love? or How do you think your Bible story today might help you through the week? or What questions do you have about your Bible lesson today? Ask questions that require children to think through the lesson and if possible to retell it. If adults are familiar with the story, a fun way to play with this concept is to make obvious errors as you tell the story. Nine times out of ten, the children will make the corrections.

Another suggestion for parents is to refer to the lesson during the week at mealtime or bedtime. This reinforcement and recall will help to develop neural pathways.

Spiritual suggestions create memories and thus bear mentioning as reinforcement:

* Say grace at meals and prayers at bedtime. Ask children to mention something they wish to pray for or to be thankful for. These activities serve a twofold purpose: (1) God is kept a viable presence in the lives of children; and (2) They are asked to recall events of importance in their day, which strengthens neural pathways.

* Take children to church—you will be amazed at what they learn even when you do not think they are paying attention.

135

* Teach children about worship and why you think it is important to attend.

* Model Christian life—don't lie and then tell them not to; you can't kid a kid!

* Read the Bible on your own and with your children.

* Make attending worship a joyous time.

* Expect good behavior, and most often you will get it.

* Teach children to be good stewards of time, money, and the earth; tell them why.

* Teach children to do for others—visit older folks, create care packages; as a family discover good causes to support, and talk about your reasons.

Life suggestions create memories and thus bear mentioning as reinforcement:

* Talk to children.

* Listen to children.

* Ask for children's opinions on daily events, and then ask the reasoning for their thinking.

* Develop critical thinking practices.

Rate everyday things on a scale of 1 to 10.

Have debates on (age-appropriate) issues.

Watch TV and commercials with a critical eye.

Ask what if? and why?

* Include children in decision making—restaurants, movies, vacation sites.

Provide choices.

Work together to set family guidelines and their reinforcement.

Expect accountability.

Determine consequences.

Learn to prioritize: select five items; then decide which one or
two you really want and why.

* Read to or with children—model the importance of reading.

* Visit museums—encourage the love of discovery.

* Travel—experience new places, foods, customs.

* Get acquainted with nature—explore local and regional parks.

* Attend plays and concerts.

* Encourage learning to play an instrument—the mental rehearsal

and discipline is what counts; do not expect a musical prodigy. (You may be surprised!)

* Sing—teach songs and make up words to tunes children know.

* Laugh—tell funny or silly jokes and stories.

* Go on a "triangle hunt"—take a walk and find as many triangles as you can (or circles, or rectangles, or colors, or sizes—big, little, tiny).

* Categorize things: buttons, leaves, coins.

* Exercise—teach children the importance of caring for their bodies.

* Eat well—avoid the junk food trap.

* Rest—children need their sleep.

Resources

Books
All books are current thinking except for a few "classics."

Armstrong, Thomas, *Awakening Your Child's Natural Genius,* New York: Putnam, 1991.

Bruce, Barbara, *7 Ways of Teaching the Bible to Children,* Nashville: Abingdon, 1996.

Bruce, Barbara, *7 Ways of Teaching the Bible to Adults,* Nashville: Abingdon, 2000.

Costa, Arthur and Kallick, Bena (ed). *Discovering and Exploring Habits of Mind,* Alexandria, Virginia: Association for Supervision and Curriculum Development, 2000.

Dennison, Gail and Dennison, Paul, *The Brain Gym,* Ventura, California: Edu-Kinesthetics, 1994.

Gardner, Howard, *Frames of Mind,* New York: Basic Books, 1983.

Gardner, Howard, *Intelligence Reframed: Multiple Intelligences for the 21st Century,* New York: Basic Books, 1999.

Gardner, Howard, *The Unschooled Mind: How Children Think and How Schools Should Teach,* New York: Basic Books, 1991.

Goldman, Robert; Klatz, Ronald; and Berger, Lisa, *Brain Fitness,* New York: Doubleday Inc., 1999.

Goleman, Daniel, *Emotional Intelligence: Why it can matter more than I.Q.,* New York: Bantam Books, 1997.

Howard, Pierce J., *The Owner's Manual for the Brain,* Marietta, Georgia: Bard Press, 2000.

Jensen, Eric, *Teaching With the Brain in Mind,* Alexandria, Virginia: Association for Supervision and Curriculum Development, 1998.

Keating, Charles, *Who We Are Is How We Pray—Matching Personality and Spirituality,* Mystic, Connecticut: Twenty Third Publications, 1988.

Michaud, Ellen and Wild, Russell (eds.), *Boost Your Brain Power,* New York: MJF Books, 1991.

Promislow, Sharon, *Making the Brain Body Connection,* West Vancouver BC, Canada: Kinetic Publishing Corporation, 1999.

Sonneman, Milly R., *Beyond Words: A Guide to Drawing Out Ideas,* Berkeley, California: Ten Speed Press, 1997.

Sylwester, Robert, *A Celebration of Neurons: An Educator's Guide to the Brain,* Alexandria, Virginia: Association for Supervision and Curriculum Development, 1995.

Titus, Harold H., *Living Issues in Philosophy,* New York: American Book Co., 1959.

Turkington, Carol, *The Brain Encyclopedia,* New York: Checkmark Books, 1999.

Westerhoff, John, *Will Our Children Have Faith?* New York: Seabury Press, 1976.

Wolfe, Patrica, *Brain Matters,* Alexandria, Virginia: Association for Supervision and Curriculum Development, 2001.

Wycoff, Joyce, *Mindmapping: Your Personal Guide to Exploring Creativity and Problem Solving,* New York: Berkley Book, 1991.

Articles From Periodicals

Caine, Renate Nummela, "Building the Bridge from Research to Classroom," *Educational Leadership*, ASCD Vol. 58 #3, November 2000, 59–61.

D'Angelo, Marcia, "The Scientist in the Crib—A Conversation With Andrew Meltzoff," *Educational Leadership*, ASCD Vol. 58 #3, November 2000, 8–13.

Greenleaf, Robert, "Developing Language: The Science Behind Learning to Read," *American Language Review*, May/June 2000.

Jensen, Eric, "Moving With the Brain in Mind," *Educational Leadership*, ASCD Vol. 58, #3, November 2000, 34–37.

Swerdlow, Joel, "Quiet Miracles of the Brain," *National Geographic*, Washington DC: Volume 187, No. 6, June 1995, 2–41.

Web Sites

www.umc.org—The United Methodist Church
www.newhorizons.com—Educational Web site with a "brain lab"
www.neuromart.com—brain stuff
www.brain.com—interesting information on all areas of brain research

Articles From the Net

Diamond, Marian, "The Brain . . . Use It or Lose It" (*www.blarg.net/~building/blab_diamond2.html*)

Diamond, Marian, "The Significance of Enrichment" (*www.blarg.net/~building/blab_diamond1.html*)

Diamond, Marian, "My Search for Love and Wisdom in the Brain" (*www.blarg.net/~building/blab_wisdom.html*)

Kotulak, Ronald, "Learning How To Use the Brain" (*www.blarg.net~building/ofc_21cliusebrain.html*)

Leiner, Henrietta and Leiner, Alan, "The Treasure at the Bottom of the Brain" (*www.blarg.net/~building/blab_leiner.html*)

Marchese, Theodore, "The New Conversations About Learning: Insights From Neuroscience and Anthropology, Cognitive Science and Work-Place Studies" (*www.aahe.org/pubs/TM-essay.htm*)

Medina, John, "The Terror of Critical Thinking and Why I Don't Believe in First Grade" (*www.blarg.net/~building/blab/fifth_medina2.htm*)

Sylwester, Robert, "The Downshifting Dilemma: A Commentary and Proposal" (*www.blarg.net/~building/blab_sylwester2.html*)

Video

PBS HOME VIDEO, *Stealing Time* - Section 3, "Mastering the Mind"